STANDARD LOAN

UNLESS RECALLED BY ANOT
THIS ITEM MAY BE BORRO

KT-489-939

Recognising Early Literacy Development:
Assessing Children's Achievements

CHICHESTER INSTITUTE OF
HIGHER EDUCATION

WS 2136203 3

AUTHOR	
NUTBROWN	
TITLE	CLASS No.
RECOGNISING	372·6

SEP96 TES

Recognising Early Literacy Development: Assessing Children's Achievements

Cathy Nutbrown

P·C·P

Paul Chapman
Publishing Ltd

Copyright © 1997 Cathy Nutbrown

All rights reserved

Paul Chapman Publishing Ltd
144 Liverpool Road
London
N1 1LA

Apart from any fair dealing for the purposes of research or
private study, or criticism or review, as permitted under the
Copyright, Designs and Patents Act, 1988, this publication may be
reproduced, stored or transmitted, in any form or by any means,
only with the prior permission in writing of the publishers, or
in the case of reprographic reproduction, in accordance with the
terms of licences issued by the Copyright Licensing Agency.
Inquiries concerning reproduction outside those terms should be
sent to the publishers at the abovementioned address.

British Library Cataloguing in Publication Data

Nutbrown, Cathy
Recognising early literacy development: assessing
children's achievements
1. Literacy 2. Literacy – Study and teaching (Elementary) –
Evaluation
I.Title
372.6

ISBN 1 85396 366 6

Typeset by Whitelaw & Palmer Ltd, Glasgow
Printed and bound in Great Britain

A B C D E F G H   9 8 7

For those who respect learning enough to assess it with integrity

and

for those who are so young that they have yet to learn
what assessment means.

Contents

Acknowledgements

The thinking which underpins this book draws on years of working with children, parents, teachers and students and this work is influenced by many who are not named here, but who through their interactions with me form part of my history of learning. My colleagues in early education continue to stimulate my thinking and I pay tribute to them for their generosity of time and expertise. The work of teachers in this book is acknowledged for its vital contribution.

As ever, Marianne Lagrange, Paul Chapman and Joyce Lynch at Paul Chapman Publishing have provided that level of professional expertise and a personal 'something' that made completing this book so pleasurable.

My many colleagues in the Division of Education at the University of Sheffield are generous in their support, but four people have played key roles in the formation of this work. I am proud to be associated with colleagues who, in different ways, have offered their specific expertise and support in the writing of this book. Kath Hirst, Elaine Millard, Nicki Hedge (now at the University of Glasgow) and Peter Hannon have my deep appreciation. They have offered their compliments and criticisms of my ideas and manuscripts with honesty, clarity and compassion. Peter Hannon has trusted my efforts over many years to improve understanding of early literacy assessment and through our many and long discussions helped me to clarify my thinking and encouraged me to seek with patience and diligence some solutions to my questions. The opportunity to work with those who value learning enough to seek to recognise and assess it with integrity is a jewel to be treasured.

Teaching, researching and writing become part of one's being, so I am equally indebted to my family (older and younger – near and far) for their unique contribution to my work.

Love of learning and love of life go together – neither can provide satisfaction alone. I am truly grateful for the 'company' I keep.

Cathy Nutbrown
Sheffield – April 1997

Foreword

This book is a result of work over many years involving assessment of young children's learning and interest in their developing literacy. Through my work as a nursery teacher I developed an understanding of the importance of building curriculum and teaching upon observations and interactions with children. In 1994 in my book *Threads of Thinking* I tried to show how teaching should be based on observations of children and curriculum should be planned around understandings of *how* children learn. Through observation, and ongoing assessment, giving close attention to children's persistent concerns, the rich content of *what* children learn can be extended. My thinking on curriculum, observation and assessment was marked in 1996 by my collaboration with several colleagues in *Respectful Educators – Capable Learners* which emphasised children's rights in early education and the role that educators can play in 'respectful assessment' of children's learning.

This record of experience in teaching and working with teachers, children and parents influenced my work throughout the 1990s on assessment of early literacy development. *Recognising Early Literacy Development* has grown from my conviction that children are entitled to be assessed in ways which respect them as people and as learners.

As a teacher I used a variety of ways to understand children's literacy. As I developed my work in the field of educational research, and as I worked with other teachers who are interested in literacy research, my concern about ways in which some researchers assessed children's literacy grew. It seemed that researchers who needed statistical data were using measures of literacy which did not match the ways teachers assessed literacy. Some tests used by researchers did not even involve children in holding a book or a pen. Did this have to be? Was there some secret about assessment for research purposes that I did not know? Why the mismatch between interesting research into early or 'emergent literacy' development and literacy measures? Why the apparent gulf between the ways teachers and researchers assessed literacy? These questions lie at the heart of *Recognising Early Literacy Development*. They were my motivation for developing work on assessment of early literacy development.

As a researcher I wanted to use measures of literacy which respected children's literacy and involved them in meaningful literacy tasks. In my search for such measures I found some existing measures to be distant from current best practice in literacy teaching and somewhat alien in their understanding of what constituted early literacy development. Many available measures used by researchers seemed a far cry from the portfolios of achievement which I kept as a nursery teacher and out of touch with the insightful ways in which teachers can assess what the children they teach know about literacy. This book traces the thinking which led to the development of a new measure. I set out to understand more about the measures that existed, a task which led me to develop a new way of assessing children's literacy. The *Sheffield Early Literacy Development Profile* is a measure of literacy designed for specific research purposes with tasks as closely matched to the best practice in teacher assessment as could be managed in a context out of the flow of everyday literacy.

I did not embark on this task lightly. Showing due respect for the richness and power of children's thinking is one of the greatest challenges for teachers and researchers who wish to assess young children's learning with integrity.

There is no better way of understanding children's learning than looking daily at their doings, listening to their words and questions and talking with their parents. If I had to choose one form of assessment this would be the one, because no test can adequately identify learning needs and therefore act as a basis for the planning of teaching. But there is room for more than one way of looking at children's learning, and certain purposes are best served by different assessment processes.

There are times when assessments other than ongoing teacher assessment are needed to provide brief profiles of children's achievement. That is where careful – and respectful – development of new assessment practices can be employed. Too many research studies have relied on poorly developed tests – constructed on questionable assumptions about what young children know or should know at a particular chronological point in their lives. What is needed for many research purposes are measures that can give a quick sketch of children's abilities to add to a bank of evidence about the effects of working with children – and their parents in different ways. Such 'sketches' are not comparable to the 'oil painting' of detail that can be obtained through a portfolio of children's achievements, but a carefully composed sketch can still tell us something worth knowing.

Those who teach, those who research and those who make and implement policy all hold stakes in the business of assessment (as they do in the business of learning). Different sections and chapters of this book will speak differently to different people depending on their perspectives.

Each will take meaning from, and bring their own meanings to, the following pages. The book is for those who have an interest in early literacy assessment: teachers who use research findings to develop their teaching; researchers who use assessments in their research, and teacher researchers who investigate their own practice and in so doing contribute to understanding of teaching and learning.

I have written *Recognising Early Literacy Development* for several reasons: to contribute to understanding of assessment of early literacy development; to provide a perspective on measures used by researchers (and increasingly by teachers); to encourage those who use early literacy measures to think about 'fitness for purpose'; and to support teachers in their thinking about purposes of early literacy assessment as they embark on a new era of national assessment of children who begin school.

Cathy Nutbrown
April 1997

1

Issues in Assessing Early Literacy Development

Introduction

Early literacy development and achievement is a controversial topic and there is much at stake. During the years three to five – before children begin compulsory schooling – their literacy can be highly developed. It is around these preschool years that there is significant, recent research in early literacy development and this growing body of research has major implications for assessment.

During the 1990s early literacy assessment became the focus of interest and with that interest came concern. A number of factors provide a context for thinking about early literacy assessment:

- the nature of literacy
- the nature of early literacy development
- historical perspectives
- the concept of *'recognition'*
- the contribution of research to early literacy and its assessment
- bilingualism and early literacy assessment
- rights and responsibilities
- parents and early literacy assessment
- the variety of approaches
- the need for new measures.

These factors are explored and explained more fully in this chapter.

The nature of literacy

One could define literacy as the ability to engage with written language. But short definitions of literacy are misleading because they gloss over its complexities and, as David Barton illustrates below, literacy processes and outcomes cannot be divorced from the range of social contexts in which they occur:

All sorts of people talk about literacy and make assumptions about it, both within education and beyond it. The business manager bemoans the lack of literacy skills in the work force. The politician wants to eradicate the scourge of illiteracy. The radical educator attempts to empower and liberate people. The literary critic sorts the good writers from the bad writers. The teacher diagnoses reading difficulties and prescribes a programme to solve them. The preschool teacher watches literacy emerge. These people all have powerful definitions of what literacy is. They have different ideas of 'the problem', and what should be done about it.

(Barton, 1994 p. 2)

Barton's point about the range of people interested in literacy is clear but one would hope to persuade him to reconsider his view of the role of preschool teachers, who do not simply 'watch literacy emerge' but actively engage in literacy with the children they teach in order to support, challenge and extend children's literacy learning!

As Hall (1987) observed, literacy is for many an essential element of everyday life:

Literacy in the Western world is a fact of everyday existence. To awake and find all print removed from the environment would be an unnerving experience. Literacy appears for many to be addictive. People take print everywhere. We take books on holidays to distant places and may even, like Somerset Maugham, carry a bag of books with us. On holiday we feel deprived if we cannot get our daily newspaper, and many people cannot sit in a room without their eyes gravitating towards print in any form. Most of us even carry around significant amounts of print in our pockets and on our clothes.

(p. 16)

Hall's view is not the case for everyone, but his point that literacy is a factor in many lives is well made. Literacy is a social construct which enables human beings to communicate. There are certain skills which accomplished users of literacy have and which new users of literacy develop in the process of literacy engagement. Formal learning settings can help people to acquire and refine such skills, as can the learning which takes place in home and community settings. Literacy as a curriculum area – like other curriculum areas – exists because literacy exists in society. The school curriculum can help children further to develop their literacy or can create blocks in children's literacy learning, disempowering children who find that their home and school literacies are different. Millard (1997a), for example, highlights issues of gender in literacy practices and illustrates that literacy (specifically reading) is constructed within home and school settings as an interest more appropriate for adolescent girls than for boys. She argues that curriculum should take account of this but that more information is needed about literacy in everyday life before curriculum change can confidently be made:

> Until we have acquired more detailed evidence of how differential access by class and race, as well as gender, to both old and new forms of literacy, continues to shape attitudes and relationships to reading and writing in school, it is difficult to set priorities for the encouragement of good classroom practice . . . more careful analysis of greater understanding of contemporary literacy practices might encourage teachers to be more critical of school's dependence on book-based learning in general, and fiction in particular, and make a greater variety of literate practices available to all pupils.
>
> (p. 46)

As Millard's work illustrates, literacy is more than reading or writing – it is embedded in the contexts in which it occurs and the meanings that they hold for individuals. Meaning connects literacy with life, and in life there are times when what literacy *accomplishes* can be more important than correct observance of its conventions.

When people read and write they do so for different reasons, their literacy is always functional – it takes place for a reason, it fulfils a need. It is difficult, perhaps impossible, to find examples of literacy in everyday life which are devoid of meaning. People write to convey a message, be it to themselves (such as a shopping list or diary entry) or to others (such as a letter or formal contract). Depending on the context the same words can mean different things: *Do not open'* handwritten on a brightly wrapped parcel can convey the meaning of a surprise which must be received at a given time. The same message in bold uppercase type '**DO NOT OPEN**' on a laboratory door can convey danger or an unwelcoming reception inside. The changing of meanings according to context is an issue for reading as well as for writing.

> Different texts are read in different ways. The same text, such as a verse from a religious text, can also be read in very different ways. It can be taken factually, as an instruction, as something to provoke meditation and thought. Often texts are reread to take further meanings. There is the possibility of oppositional readings.
>
> (Barton, 1994 p. 65)

Though discussion here focuses on literacy, the implicit connection of literacy and oracy needs to be acknowledged. Reading and writing, speaking and listening are functions of language – the elements of literacy being linked to those that comprise oracy. The important feature of language – written and spoken – is that it fulfils the need human beings have to communicate. Literacy and oracy are interlinked. People make choices in their daily interactions with others about which functions of language they will use. Such choices can depend upon the purpose of the interaction and factors of meaning and function can influence decisions about whether to speak or whether to write (or whether to do both). Hall's view of the interrelationship between literacy and oracy emphasised meaning and function:

> Literacy, like oral language, exists so that meanings can be created and so that communication can take place between human beings. Literacy events are, like oral language events, experienced as meaningful and are usually experienced as means to various ends. Most importantly, literacy, like oral language, is experienced as having many uses and functions because it enables the achievement of that variety of ends.
>
> (Hall, 1987, p. 16)

A holistic overview of teaching literacy and of research in literacy is useful, but this is not to say that there cannot be times when particular parts of the whole come more sharply into view. This book focuses specifically on literacy, and on the literacy of children before the age of five.

The nature of early literacy

There is controversy even over the definition of early literacy development. Clear understanding of what constitutes early literacy development and knowledge of underpinning assumptions and theories is therefore essential if other issues in the achievement of early literacy development are to be properly addressed.

Over the past two decades, there has been a change in the way that early literacy development has been seen. It is now widely recognised that literacy begins and can be promoted in the preschool years (in the UK that is up to the age of five). Children born into a world full of print try to make sense of it while they are very young, in the context of their day-to-day lives at home and in the community.

The teaching of literacy was once widely assumed to be the domain of the school, with the dominant idea that children had to be taught specifically defined 'pre-reading skills' in a distinct manner. Walker (1975) for example, argued that: 'success in the skills of reading depends on successful acquisition of the related subskills of pre-reading' (p. 7).

He continued his argument by emphasising the importance of first developing mainly perceptual skills such as: shape and letter discrimination, hand-eye co-ordination, left-right eye movements, visual memory, listening and auditory skills, phonemic discrimination, auditory memory, letter recognition and knowledge of letter names and sounds. Referring to this list of skills he wrote:

> in order to overcome the unique difficulties inherent in beginning reading it is necessary for the child to have first developed a minimum set of skills and capacities.
>
> (ibid. p. 7)

The perspective of literacy which some have termed *emergent literacy* (Teale and Sulzby, 1986; Hall, 1987) has helped us to a different view of early literacy development. Yetta Goodman (1980) wrote about the *roots* of literacy developing in the preschool period as including:

- print awareness in situational contexts
- awareness of connected discourse in written language
- meta cognitive and meta linguistic awareness about written language
- using oral language about written language
- functions and forms of writing.

For healthy growth she suggests these roots need the fertile soil of a literate environment:

- symbol systems – as in art, music and dance
- variety of functions of written language
- adult language about written language
- oral language development
- background – something upon which to build
- experience which aids development.

The *emergent literacy* perspective on early literacy shows how much very young children know about reading and writing. For example:

- recognising, making sense of and using their knowledge and under-standing of print in the environment
- sharing books with adults
- being *apprentices* to adult literacy experiences in the home
  - sitting on a parent's knee as he or she reads the paper
  - writing shopping lists
  - sending and receiving cards and letters
- early scribble and drawing, and early attempts at writing, gradually developing into conventional writing
- using knowledge about literacy in socio-dramatic play.

Literacy skills such as book handling, writing conventions, and letter knowledge can be taught and reinforced from a developmental view-point, as part of meaningful literacy experiences. Such experiences can be used to teach and reinforce specific skills too, and *meaning* (such as is present in much home literacy) is also crucial in *planned* teaching. Children's spontaneous early literacy activities are meaningful and rele-vant to them (even if adults do not recognise their efforts as having the sophistication of adult literacy), because they arise from what the children have so far understood about literacy, by a process of drawing from literacy they see and take part in.

Kenneth Goodman (1986) has argued that *function* matters more than *form*. That is to say – it is important first for children to be able to make their literacy do what they want it to do. Through engagement with the *functions* of literacy Goodman argues that children are motivated to get control of the *form* of language, how it works, its constituent parts and rules: 'language is easy to learn if it meets a functional need the child feels' (p. 18).

As well as function before form, the idea of literacy learning as *whole* to *part* is also important from the emergent literacy perspective. Goodman argues that language is learned *as a whole* and it is only later that we see and develop and understand the parts. He wrote:

> The whole is always more than the sum of the parts and the value of any part can only be learned within the whole utterance in a real speech event.
>
> (ibid. p. 19)

This perspective on early literacy development places meaning and function before accuracy and convention, and from this theoretical position it could be argued that when children have a sense of meanings and functions in literacy they are spurred on to tackle some parts of the conventions of literacy.

Emergent literacy gives us a clear view of the importance of several factors, including:

- connections between reading and writing
- the role of children's families
- play as a way of rehearsing and developing literacy skills and understandings
- the place of context and meaning.
- effective ways of teaching specific literacy skills.

Emergent or developmental literacy supposes that children, before they go to school, are active in their pursuit of literacy skills, knowledge and understanding, and that, in so doing, they have generated a positive view of literacy. They often see literacy as exciting, interesting, a 'good thing' to get involved in and something they *can* do.

This particular perspective on early literacy development is still evolving and, as with any theoretical position, there is an inevitably provisional nature to it. New perspectives evolve which lead to the reappraisal of existing research and which inform the development of future research. One example of this was the work of Ferrerio and Teberosky (1982) whose research focused on children's writing. This research shed new light on children's construction of personal spelling rules and in so doing contributed to the development of a theoretical view of children as competent learners of writing systems and to an approach to researching the development of writing that might be adopted in the future. Ferrerio and Teberosky proposed a view of the 'evolution of writing' and of children posing their own literacy problems which they are motivated to solve. In terms of reading, Ferrerio and Teberosky concluded that reading is not deciphering and challenged skills based approaches to teaching reading. They argued that children who only learned to decipher print had a limited view of reading and a limited reading ability. Children who, according to Ferrerio and Teberosky 'have organised their own learning' are readers in the fullest sense of the term, having mastery of processes and skills of reading as well as a sense of its purposes and pleasures. Such a stance on early literacy learning requires reconsideration of previous studies and of the way early literacy is viewed.

Examples of the importance of meaning, of home literacy, of play, and of context can be found in children's play which involves literacy. Nigel Hall (1991) suggested that:

> Play offers an opportunity to help children preserve the wider understanding of literacy by allowing them the chance to explore literacy in contextualised situations.

> (p. 11)

Simply giving children literacy related materials and the opportunity to play is of limited use unless they also have some sense of *how* to use them, derived from experiences of the reality of literacy in different situations. Wray *et al.* (1989) suggest children need to see literacy happening:

> A literate environment is a fairly meaningless concept without people who are using that environment, people who, through a variety of ways in which they use print, demonstrate when it is used, how it is used, where it is used and what it is.

> (p. 66)

For preschool children, written language can be a significant part of their worlds and some will notice that it is a significant part of the world of their parents or other family members. It is as natural for them to be curious about it, to ask questions, and to want to talk about it from time to time, as about other matters that interest and confront them. Children's vocabularies grow rapidly in the preschool years; it follows that, during the processes of playing with and talking about literacy with peers and with adults, children will acquire new words about written language. This kind of literacy vocabulary can be used to discuss their literacy, the content of stories and the attributes of authors and illustrators (Nutbrown and Hannon, 1997).

Emergent literacy development includes peaks and plateaus. It is not always easy to plot progress in a neat and upward rising line. Like all development, there are slow as well as rapid periods – times of process with no obvious product and occasions of accelerated progress can be juxtaposed with apparent regression.

Historical perspectives

Thinking today (or until recently – lack of thinking) about early literacy assessment can be accounted for in historical terms. The way literacy in children's early years has been perceived has impacted upon the current need for better assessment.

Until the early 1980s there was a tradition of professional reluctance amongst nursery teachers to teach literacy to preschool children. As Hannon (1995) notes:

> They have tended to resist pressures from parents and teachers of older children to 'start children off early' in reading and writing. In the past, some eradicated print from the nursery environment and emphasised alternatives to literacy – pictures not words, paint brushes not pens, pictures of animals, flowers or toys in place of children's names in the cloakroom.
>
> (p. 55)

It is likely that this extreme practice was rooted in two things:

- a desire to shield children from tedious decontextualised 'pre-reading' and 'pre-writing' exercises, empty of meaning
- a desire to preserve the importance of play and social interaction in early childhood education.

As Chapter 2 will demonstrate, things have changed, but given the philosophy of 'no literacy in the nursery' perpetuated throughout the 1960s and 1970s (Hodgson, 1987), it is not surprising that literacy assessment has, only recently, featured on the early education agenda.

The concept of 'recognition'

One way of improving assessment is to *recognise* children's literacy achievements. Recent research focusing on parents' roles in children's literacy (Hannon, 1995; Nutbrown and Hannon, 1997) has introduced the concept of 'recognition' – adults who share literacy with children being in a better position to show 'recognition' of children's achievements.

'Recognition' of children's achievements comes when adults can identify and acknowledge developmental literacy milestones and literacy efforts of young children. Hannon (1995) uses the term 'recognition' as one of four elements of the parents' role in early literacy development:

> The importance of the parent's role can be understood in terms of four things they can provide for developing readers and writers: *opportunities* for learning, *recognition* of the child's achievements, *interaction* around literacy activities, and a *model* of literacy.
>
> (p. 51)

The concept of recognition has been further employed in the REAL – Raising Early Achievement in Literacy Project (Nutbrown and Hannon, 1997) which, in conjunction with teachers, has developed ways of working with parents to enhance their recognition of children's development in four key strands of early literacy: environmental print, books, writing and oral language. Nutbrown and Hannon emphasise the importance of working with parents to enhance their recognition of each of these aspects of early literacy. Discussing environmental print, for example, they write:

> The very act of identifying the things they see their children doing can act as a reminder for parents to show recognition of their child's use of environmental print the next time it happens and can highlight the importance of new learning that may come later.
>
> (Nutbrown and Hannon, 1997, p. 93)

'Recognition' of early literacy development requires knowledge about early literacy development and skills of observation and assessment, to be able first to identify children's literacy achievements *as achievements* (however small), and second to 'recognise' them with the child. This can involve such actions as:

- discussing the achievement
- making a note of it
- telling someone else
- praising or encouraging the child
- saving writing
- drawing the child's attention to the significance of what he or she has done.

This concept of 'recognition', broadened to include teachers, researchers and policy makers, underpins much of the thinking in this book. After slow but eventual recognition that early literacy *exists*, there is now an urgent need to appraise existing assessment tools and ensure that, in developing new methods of assessment, proper respect for young children and fuller recognition of their literacy is shown.

The contribution of research

Research studies have made a significant contribution to understanding how early literacy is learned, and how it can be better taught and discussed. Research also has a key role to play in the development of appropriate *assessment* tools.

Key research into early literacy development has taught us much about how young children learn to be literate, and about the stages of progression from early discoveries to later capabilities and understanding about words, print, books and other elements of literacy (Ferrerio and Teberosky, 1982; Sulzby 1985a; Goodman, 1980). Some researchers

(Durkin, 1966; Payton, 1984; Bissex, 1980) have observed children, considered their early writing and made judgements about their ability and their skills in literacy. Observation and inference are the main methods of describing early literacy development and there are some well documented descriptions of children taking their early steps along the literacy road (Butler, 1979; Payton, 1984; Bissex, 1980, Schickedanz 1990). These studies contain insights about children developing their literacy which illuminate ideas about emergent literacy, inexplicable without consideration of home learning. Chapters 2 and 4 continue the theme of the contribution of research to early literacy development and its assessment.

Bilingualism and early literacy assessment

Many young children in school in the UK are from bilingual or multilingual families. How their early literacy is assessed is worthy of consideration – what counts as literacy in nursery and reception classes in the UK must not exclude literacy that is not 'English literacy'.

Early biliteracy development is not the focus of this book but it would be irresponsible not to mention the importance of taking account of bilingualism or emerging bilingualism in early literacy assessment. Keel (1994) focuses on a range of issues in the assessment of bilingual children and in so doing points to the need for further research, understanding and action to improve the assessment of children for whom English is a second language. Though this is an under researched area, bilingualism and early literacy studies do exist and they draw attention to some key issues. Hirst (1997) highlights three main points that should be born in mind when young children's biliteracy development is considered:

- bilingual families and children should not be seen as 'deficient' in literacy and language development
- it is possible to learn two oral languages and their written versions simultaneously
- what happens in bilingual homes needs to be valued

(p. 16)

In a study of bilingual Pakistani children's early literacy development, Huss (1991) found that children's homes were rich in literacy but their teachers were not attempting to understand bilingual children's 'out of school' literacy. Teachers underestimated these children's literacy because their non-English literacy was not included in the picture. As Hirst (1997) argues, bilingual children's home literacy should be taken into account when teachers make judgements about their literacy ability. Literacy ability in English may not be (and often *is* not) the sum total of bilingual children's early literacy capabilities. Other writers have also warned of the 'dangerous assumptions' of deficit that arise from inappropriate assessments of bilingual pupils (Gravelle and Sturman, 1994).

Siraj-Blatchford (1996) sets out six levels of equal opportunities practice, level '0' being the least desirable and level '5' being a state of practice that seeks to challenge inequality and promote respect. Siraj-Blatchford suggests that it is at level 5 that 'staff actively try to change the structures and power relations which inhibit equal opportunities' practice that identifies this level of working includes the following:

- bi/multilingualism is actively supported
- Equality issues are reflected across curriculum, resources, assessment and record-keeping and the general ethos of the centre

(p. 33)

With specific reference to work with children at Key Stage 1, Robson (1995) lists ten issues to consider in the assessment of bilingual pupils. This includes the point that

In the school based assessment procedure we should examine critically whether . . . the curriculum and instruction offered to the pupil is compatible with our knowledge of the way people acquire language and other cognitive skills

(p. 45)

Discussing the assessment of oral language at Key Stage 1, Mills (1995) is concerned with the question of 'fairness'. She states that an assessment is only fair if it is acknowledged that assessment of standard English is only one dimension of a child's all-round language abilities and writes:

Some children have abilities which are only apparent in one language. Many of us have had experience of meeting children who are monosyllabic in English but can carry out lengthy and involved conversations in another tongue, or children who are very able in English but cannot communicate well in their first language. Similarly, some children have abilities which transfer across language boundaries; they can describe, report incidents, and tell stories in two languages.

(p. 144)

Gregory (1996) draws attention to the 'hurdles in achieving fair assessment' of bilingual pupils. She describes the developing biliteracy of eight year old Nazma who can converse with her classmates and understand classroom discussions but remains *vulnerable* when presented with children's literature. Gregory concludes:

The question of how to provide a fair assessment for children like Nazma has not yet been answered but the obvious difficulties of the task have persuaded many countries to exclude emergent bilinguals from the language tests until they are viewed as proficient in the new language.

(p. 175)

Any single assessment provides only part of a picture. Those working with bilingual children, whether they form the majority or minority of pupils in their classrooms or nurseries, have an additional responsibility in the assessment of those children, for there is more to assess and more for their teachers to learn about. Different assessment tools are needed for different purposes and bilingual children's literacy development provides an example of the need to tailor assessment to the purpose for which it is required. To find out about achievement in English it is appropriate to assess in English; to complete the picture of a child's all round biliteracy development other assessments and processes will need to be used.

Rights and responsibilities

Adults have clear and serious responsibilities in terms of literacy assessment and, in carrying out those responsibilities, are charged with respecting children's rights to 'respectful assessment'. Those who devise assessment processes and those who carry out assessments must not underestimate, misuse or abuse their power.

Issues of 'rights' and 'responsibilities' are fundamental to this discussion of early literacy assessment. According to the UN Convention on the Rights of the Child adopted by the General Assembly of the United Nations on 20 November 1989, children have a right to be taught according to their need and in ways which enable them to reach their potential. The Convention, ratified by the UK government in December 1991, recognises children's rights to be free to communicate in a variety of forms. This has a direct link with their right to be literate. Literacy then, is the right of every child; with its acquisition comes information, knowledge and power to take one's place in society, to learn about it and the people who make it and to challenge and contribute to decisions that shape society's development. To be literate is to have a power source and children in the early years of their literacy learning can begin to build up their literacy powers.

Teaching that enables children to reach their potential requires good assessment processes. Assessment of a learner's present knowing is a sound basis for the next teaching plans. The development, implementation and evaluation of effective assessment in the classroom is the responsibility of the adults who work with and for children and education, including teachers, researchers and policy makers. In terms of assessing early literacy development it is therefore a case of children's rights and adults' responsibilities.

Drummond (1993) wrote of the assessment of children's learning in terms of rights, responsibilities and power. She recalls the work of a group of teachers on an Educational Studies course who were engaged in an exercise to identify their responsibilities to their pupils. Having identified their responsibility the teachers identified another imperative:

which would be needed to complement the concept of responsibility: the need to affirm our ability to meet our responsibilities to the height of our professional powers.

(p. 169)

The power of assessors can be infinite and ultimate. In educational assessment from a beginning in the preschool period to the highest academic qualifications, assessors and systems have power over those who are being assessed. From assessments of the preschool child to the PhD candidate, systems and assessors must show respect for learners – to the extent that they acknowledge and use their power with respect for what others know and with a disposition to appreciate when they themselves have more to learn. Nutbrown (1996) argues that children have the right to respectful assessment and adults have the responsibility to provide it. The expertise of the teacher is a crucial part of that responsibility:

> Adult knowledge is crucial to extending children's learning and essential if children's early achievements are to be recognised and respected.

(p. 54)

The concept of 'respectful assessment' is introduced as a way of achieving a variety of assessment approaches that fit the purpose:

> Respectful assessment takes account of a range of factors and achievements, values the participation of the person being assessed as well as the perspectives of those carrying out the assessment. It includes self-assessment and collaborative assessment as well as assessment of one person by someone else.

(ibid. p. 52)

Unfortunately, the Chief Inspector of Schools considered this way of describing assessment an 'impossible ideal' (Woodhead, 1997). This makes it all the more important for teachers and researchers to take account of the rights of learners and to use their their responsibilities with respect. If the power of those involved in developing, administering and reporting assessments is denied, there remains the danger that assessment processes will ride rough-shod over children's learning and development, and in so doing, miss much of what children can do.

This book highlights the inadequacies of some existing measures of literacy and argues that, for certain purposes, new assessment instruments may need to be developed. The challenge is to develop new measures of early literacy development that:

- value early literacy achievements
- respect the ways in which literacy develops
- acknowledge the rights of children to respectful assessment
- acknowledge the respective responsibilities of researchers, teachers,

and policy makers in the implementation of such assessments
* do not abuse children by misuse of the power held by assessors or those who devise assessment tools.

Parents and early literacy assessment

Issues of early literacy assessment are not solely the domain of professionals. They are the concern of parents too – the people from whom young children learn much of their literacy in the preschool years. Parents have a distinct contribution to make to the assessment of children's early literacy and some instruments have been successful in including parents in literacy assessment (Barrs *et al.* 1989).

The School Curriculum and Assessment Authority (1996a) described parental involvement as a feature of good practice. With particular reference to assessment it identified good practice taking place when:

> Children's progress and future learning needs are assessed and recorded through frequent observation and are shared regularly with parents
>
> (p. 6)

But professionals *sharing* what they have noticed with parents is only part of the picture. Parents know much about their children's literacy learning and many parents are in a position to give teachers extra insights into their children's early literacy, such as :

* the books they most enjoy
* the environmental print they recognise
* the writing events they share in and often initiate at home
* the rhymes they know well.

The REAL (Raising Early Achievement in Literacy) Project has developed four developmental jigsaws that help parents to identify the elements of literacy that their children are involved in and use at home (Nutbrown and Hannon, 1997). These jigsaws, focusing on four strands of literacy development – environmental print, books, writing and key aspects of oral language – locate assessment of early literacy development with children's parents and put them in the position of sharing what they know with their child's teachers.

Ongoing assessment for the purposes of teaching and learning is incomplete without some contribution from parents. What children do in an educational setting is only part of their profile – just as a formal assessment can only provide a part of the picture. Home literacy and home learning as observed by parents can give teachers a clearer, more holistic image of a child's all round literacy development.

A variety of approaches

One of the principles on which this book is built is that there must be a *variety* of high quality approaches for a variety of assessment *purposes*.

Descriptive observation such as that done by Durkin (1966), Payton (1984) and Bissex (1980) is crucial for teachers who work with children over a sustained period of time, but this is not always suitable for some research which requires measurement of early literacy development in a short period. Descriptions depend on the observation skills of observers, their knowledge of the situation they see, and the criteria they apply. There are times when more criterion based measures of early literacy development could be useful, for example:

- to demonstrate the effectiveness of a particular teaching strategy
- to challenge unreliable claims about standards
- to ascertain the efficacy of a research intervention study.

It is difficult, however, to assess quickly and reliably the emerging concepts and understanding of children's early literacy development. Chapter 2 further confirms this problem, showing a lack of published measurement tools for early literacy development compared with measures of older children's development.

The need for new measures

In order to attain the variety described above new measures are needed. Chapter 4 reviews three decades of measuring, assessing and recording early literacy and evaluates some assessment instruments. The purposes of literacy assessment (Chapter 5) and insight into purpose and practice of literacy assessment in schools (Chapter 6) lead to the conclusion that there is a problem in early literacy assessment, but that it lies with *researchers*, not with teachers. Some research studies have successfully developed and promoted new views of early literacy development which many teachers have found attractive and effective. Many teachers, inspired by research, have developed and adopted new teaching methods and styles, and have gone on to devise ways of assessing children's early literacy development which match these changes. Much research, however, has not kept pace with this change in literacy teaching. Instead research which uses tests continues to rely on old and often inappropriate tests, or researchers develop *ad hoc* and idiosyncratic tests. This presents a problem for anyone studying, for example, early literacy development using comparison or control groups or for researchers interested in predictors of literacy achievements.

This book considers what currently exists to assess early literacy development and illuminates a gap between research in early literacy development and its assessment. The following chapters argue that the responsibility for addressing this problem lies mainly with researchers, who must keep pace with the way in which teachers are using research to develop curriculum and ongoing assessment strategies.

2

New Views of Early Literacy Development and the Need for Measurement

Until the 1970s early literacy development had been largely overlooked. Nursery education in the UK had, on the whole, overlooked the existence of any literacy abilities in children under five years old and concentrated instead on social and emotional development and promoting spoken language (Tough, 1976; Taylor *et al.*, 1972; Hannon and James, 1990). This chapter will look at the recent history of research and practice in early literacy development, and through this identify the need for further work into how it is assessed.

Strands of research in early literacy

Hannon (1995) has suggested that early literacy development can be thought of as having three main strands: reading, writing, and oral language. Hannon sees these strands largely as a matter of convenience. He writes:

> It is . . . helpful, for practical reasons, to distinguish the three strands of literacy development . . . children's experiences of reading (environmental print as well as books and other texts), or writing, and or oral language (to include storytelling, phonological awareness and decontextualised talk).

(p. 52)

What Hannon identified as strands of early literacy *development* can perhaps be seen more usefully as strands of early literacy *research*. It is worth reflecting on how strands of early literacy research have developed, and how understanding of early literacy development has changed as a result of such research.

Research into early literacy development seems to have developed rather unevenly. Use of *books* was an early focus, then followed interest in the development of *writing*. Later research focused on children's perceptions and abilities to recognise and learn to read some *environmental print*. *Oral language* has been a continuing focus of interest but at different times the emphasis has been on different aspects (such as talk, storytelling, or phonological awareness).

Briefly, the historical origins of the three more specifically literacy strands of research (into book reading, writing and environmental print) can be attributed to three researchers. The work of Durkin (1966) in the USA began discussion on young children's ability to read books and later Clay (1975) in New Zealand stimulated two decades of research which shed new light on the early reading and writing capabilities of young children. It was Goodman (1980) who added the third strand of literacy research with her work on children's recognition and understanding of print found in the context of their environment. So far as research into elements of oral language that contribute to literacy development, the work of Bradley and Bryant (1983, 1985) and of Goswami and Bryant (1990) shed light on children's phonological awareness and Wells (1987) illuminated interest in children's storytelling and the importance of listening to stories as well as having stories read.

At the start of the 1970s new perspectives on early literacy development emerged. These were important firstly because they acknowledged the view that young children were literate and had literacy capabilities, and secondly because teachers found the research of use in their work with children in the preschool period.

Changes in the teaching of early literacy

To understand fully the impact of research in early literacy development (and key aspects of oral language) it is important to take an historical perspective. This highlights the changes that have taken place in the teaching of literacy (sharing and reading books, early writing and environmental print) and enables the identification of the role of research in those changes.

Sharing and reading books

Reading was the first strand of literacy to have a place in children's formal learning. Environmental print was very limited and reading was often confined to religious learning. In 1805 Andrew Bell, who became the superintendent of the 'National Society' which promoted church schools for the poor, argued that children should be taught to read the Bible (Simon, 1960). The literary tradition of the nineteenth century suggests that reading, for those who had the opportunity to learn, was often a traumatic and laborious process:

> I struggled through the alphabet as if it had been a bramble-bush; getting considerably worried and scratched by every letter. After

that I fell among those thieves, the nine figures, who seemed every evening to disguise themselves and baffle recognition. But, at last I began, in a purblind groping way, to read, write and cipher, on the very smallest scale.

(Pip in *Great Expectations*, Chapter 7, Dickens, 1860)

The means by which pupils in the nineteenth century were taught to read seem to have left a legacy for teachers and children in the present day which led Waterland (1992) to consider the introduction of the reading scheme:

The idea that some special sort of book was necessary really began with the introduction of elementary schooling for all in the late 1800s . . . Reading schemes were brought in to enable the untrained monitor to teach reading. These youngsters, themselves often only a very little older and wiser than those they taught, needed something which would deskill the reading process and break it down into easily passed chunks.

(p. 162)

The research of the late 1960s and early 1970s inevitably seemed to have an effect on the teaching of reading at about that time. In the UK, the 1970s saw a development in the teaching of reading when children were gradually offered more interesting reading materials as publishers of reading schemes began to update their material (Root, 1986). There was still, however, a divide between books for learning to read ('reading scheme books') and other children's books. This was not unique to the UK, a similar situation was to be found in the USA, with a clear division between 'trade books' bought from shops and read at home, and the 'basal readers' used in school.

Though there were many reading tests in use during the 1970s and 1980s, assessment of reading for the purposes of teaching and learning in the early years of school was apparently under developed. Assessment was largely based on the stages children reached on the reading scheme, their reading ability being classified according to the number of the book they were reading. This was not dissimilar to the practice established some 100 years earlier by the introduction of the Revised Code of 1862 which set out 'standards' based on the reading of 'reading-books used in the school' (Birchenough, 1914).

The 1980s saw a further development in the teaching of reading with the use of 'real books' rather than those produced for reading schemes (Waterland, 1985). Using children's literature to teach reading, rather than a commercially produced reading scheme, demanded more of teachers. It required them to know much more about *how* young children learn to read, to think about which books best supported children's learning and to develop effective teaching strategies. Teaching reading through the use of children's literature also necessitated a different way of *recognising* and *recording* reading achievement. These were challenges that many teachers were excited by and their interest in the *processes* of literacy development (as opposed to *outcomes* alone) was highlighted.

Waterland (1985) advocated an 'apprenticeship' approach to reading in which children learned to read by sharing books with an adult. Those who developed this approach demonstrated their own love of reading to children through introducing different ways of using books and through sharing stories. Such teachers found new ways of extending children's interest in literature through talking about the books they read together.

The 'apprenticeship' approach of learning to read was a concept borrowed from the model of apprenticeship in industry a century before where a young man would learn to be a carpenter (or some other trade) by becoming an apprentice to and working alongside a skilled craftsman in the workshop. In Frank Smith's terms children learning to read through apprenticeship teaching processes were 'joining the literacy club' (Smith, 1988).

Books have always been part of nursery environments but new ways of teaching reading in the early compulsory years of schooling may have been responsible for renewed interest in promoting books and stories with preschool age children. Waterland's apprenticeship approach to the teaching of reading highlighted the need for a new way of observing and recording children's progress in reading. As more schools developed their teaching of reading, often incorporating children's literature into a mixture of 'reading scheme books', more examples of new assessment procedures developed by teachers emerged (Waterland, 1989).

This new 'apprenticeship' approach to teaching reading was built upon knowledge of how young children could learn to read and demanded a high level of professional development and support. Those teachers who received the support they needed and who understood the theoretical underpinning of teaching reading through children's literature were able to develop the approach successfully with children in their classes loving reading, and behaving like readers, as well as learning *how* to read. Some teachers were not offered the new level of professional development that these appropriate teaching strategies demanded and so teaching reading through 'real books' is now – for some – a casualty of that omission.

Writing

Writing was not part of the curriculum for the poor in the early Sunday Schools of the 1800s. In 1805 Andrew Bell made his position on the role of church schools in relation to literacy clear when he wrote:

> It is not proposed that the children of the poor be educated in an expensive manner, or even taught to write and cypher.
>
> (Simon, 1960, p. 133)

The place of writing in the 'Revised Code' of 1862 was limited to copying and dictation, but not *creating* written text (Birchenough, 1914).

The National Primary Survey (DES, 1978) showed that the teaching of writing in the 1970s tended to be 'skills based' and that writing was frequently taught in the absence of context and purpose. Much of the writing children did was controlled by teachers, with content springing from teachers' ideas rather than from children's lively minds. This seemed to change rapidly in the next decade and HMI (DES, 1990b), reflecting on the teaching of literacy in the 1980s, considered it good practice to encourage children aged three and four years old to engage in play situations where they wrote letters and addressed envelopes – for example, as part of play in the classroom post office.

During the 1970s and 1980s researchers in the UK and USA, working independently, reported studies of their own children. Their detailed accounts of children in the preschool period and beyond demonstrated young children's developing literacy skills, knowledge and understanding, and a positive attitude to literacy related activities (Payton, 1984; Baghban, 1984; Bissex, 1980; Butler, 1979). Research and Government reports seemed in agreement at this time. In the UK, HMI, referring to the practice of teachers which they had observed, reported that:

> They (the children) were able to put into practice what they had noticed about letter formation, how English writing moves from left to right, and the structures and shapes of writing. They were able to experience the satisfaction of using writing to draw a response from others.
>
> (DES, 1990b, para 29)

This apparent shift in philosophy was also reflected in the work of teachers through the development of the National Writing Project (1985–1989). Originally intended to focus on writing in the statutory years of schooling (5–16 years) the project, following interest of nursery teachers, rapidly moved to include writing in the preschool period. One nursery teacher wrote:

> Writing in the nursery? My first reaction was, 'Oh no!' I felt that pressures came to the children soon enough in school and should not be introduced into the nursery. Now I have discovered that play activities can be broadened and extended by providing the opportunity for some form of writing.
>
> (Hodgson, 1987, p. 11)

In 1988 the DES further recognised that young children were capable of early writing and that this began before some children attended school:

> Just as many young children come to school believing that they can read, so they will come willingly to try to write. This may at first be

simple 'draw writing' but as they develop and learn more about how written language works, their writing comes increasingly close to standard adult systems.

(DES, 1988, para 10.12)

At the start of the 1990s, current research, government policy and practice in schools seemed in some agreement. There was evidence in policy documents of recognition of strands of early literacy research which were exemplified by observations of classroom practice. We now need to look at developments with regard to the third strand of early literacy development, that is children's awareness and developing knowledge of literacy through interacting with print in the environment, such as advertisements, signs and notices.

Environmental print

Relatively unheard of until Goodman's work (1980), and made popular by teachers through the work of the National Writing Project (1989), was the belief that children learned something about print by living in a literate and print rich environment. There are many examples of teachers using logos and familiar words from the environment to help children to learn more about literacy (Hall, 1989; Hall and Abbott, 1991; Nutbrown and Hannon, 1997).

In a study of children's ability to read ten items of functional environmental print McGee, Lomax and Head (1984) found that:

Children attend to all sorts of print that surrounds them in a highly meaningful way. Not only do they know the type of print-conveyed meaning associated with different print items performing different literacy functions, but they also are sensitive to the language cues, including graphic detail, in written language.

(p. 15)

HMI (DES, 1989) acknowledged the importance of environmental print in the development of young children's literacy:

Children are well used to seeing print in the home, in the streets, in the supermarket and in a variety of other places they visit with their parents. Many of them already have an interest in reading, some are readers already, and teachers of young children seek to sustain and develop this skill at a pace appropriate to each child.

(para 32)

This is an approach to teaching literacy far removed from the education of Dickens' day and the Revised Code of 1862. It is an approach which current research has both stimulated and supported and one which many teachers of young children have maximised in terms of the curriculum opportunities it opens up.

Key aspects of oral language

There has always been an emphasis on the development of oral language in early childhood education, but perhaps it has not always been clear which aspects of *oral* language contribute to *literacy* development. Written language is a way of representing the sounds of the words used in *speech*. Using *written* language presupposes some knowledge of the sound structure of oral language. The specific focus of knowledge of *oral* language is crucial, as subskills, such as knowing the sounds that the 26 letters of the English alphabet supposedly 'make', are of minimal use here. Neither does it help children to read to know that letter 'N' can represent 'nuh' if that sound cannot be 'heard' in a word such as 'string'. Another approach is to consider 'sound awareness' as a factor that could help literacy development. Linguists break oral language down into units called 'phonemes' (there are supposedly 44 in the English language) and *phonemic awareness* is considered helpful in reading and spelling. However, phonemes are often difficult to spot, and phonemic awareness may be acquired as a result of becoming literate, rather than something which helps children to become literate.

Research suggests that key aspects of oral language have an impact on children's literacy learning and development, particularly phonological awareness and storytelling. These can be considered strong elements of the oral language strand of literacy development.

Phonological awareness

In the 1980s the work of Peter Bryant, Lynette Bradley and Usha Goswami, helped to pinpoint the importance of *phonological awareness* in children's literacy development. Goswami and Bryant (1990) stressed the importance of children's awareness of beginning and end sounds – *onset* and *rime* – in spoken words. They argued that preschool children who are aware of onset and rime find learning to read easier, their literacy being enhanced if children can identify, for example, similar onsets such as in : 'strong', 'stretch', and 'stripe' and similar rimes as in: 'wing', 'thing', 'ring', and 'beginning'. Goswami and Bryant demonstrate that preschool tests of this kind of phonological awareness could be used to predict reading attainment later and showed that preschool 'training' to help children identify onset and rime could enhance later reading attainment. Maclean, Bryant and Bradley (1987) found that the number of *nursery rhymes* known by preschool children predicted later reading success in school. Children could become aware that words have different parts through singing and saying rhymes which repeat words with the same onsets or rimes.

Storytelling

Well's longitudinal study (1987) revealed four experiences of language in the home which he considered might be important to children's later reading achievement. These were: listening to a story; other sharing of picture books; drawing and colouring; and early writing. Of these four, *listening to stories read aloud* stood out above the others as being related to later achievement in school. Wells suggested the reasons for this centred around the various benefits children gain from *listening* to stories:

- experience of a genre later encountered in written form
- extension of experience and vocabulary
- increased conversation with adult
- child's own 'inner storying' validated
- experience of language use to *create worlds*
- insight into *storying* as means of understanding.

Others, such as Margaret Meek (1989) and Jerome Bruner (1991) have emphasised the importance of story in the development of literacy and in thinking.

The need for measurement

With new views of early literacy development developing from an increasing body of research in the field (Holdaway, 1979; Temple *et al.*, 1982; Ferrerio and Teberosky, 1982, Harste *et al.*, 1984) teachers were able to support and extend children's literacy development from a young age (e.g. Manchester Literacy Project, 1988; National Writing Project, 1989; Sheffield Early Years Literacy Association, 1991).

Once such an approach to literacy development was admitted, it gained popularity during the 1970s and 1980s, and prompted questions of how best to measure this newly acknowledged behaviour. Formats and processes for teacher assessments were developed (e.g. Manchester, 1988; Barrs *et al.*, 1989; Waterland, 1989; Chittenden and Courtney, 1989). Despite a growth of interest in literacy in the UK and innovative international research into reading and writing during the same period (Clay, 1975; Goodman, 1980; Ferrerio and Teberosky, 1982) specific *measures* of literacy which reflect these research interests and which could be used for research involving comparisons are still in short supply.

Whilst research focused increasingly on 'emergent literacy' and children's developing knowledge and understanding of environmental print, books and stories, and early writing behaviours, measurement of children's behaviour was restricted to tests of vocabulary, visual discrimination, and other related (but isolated) skills.

Even though researchers were watching children and understanding more of how they learned and even though teachers were using and developing the implications of this new knowledge, some studies of children's literacy ability still relied on tests which (on the face of it at least) had at best only tenuous links with children's literacy. Tests focused on 'prerequisites' for literacy: capabilities in visual discrimination, one to one correspondence, and matching colours, shapes and pictures – but showed little recognition of children's *actual* literacy interests. Such skills were all considered predictors of later literacy ability, and the teaching of 'prereading' skills was once seen as an essential role of teachers in nursery and early infant classes:

> Prereading comprises all the many activities and skills that the child will need **before** the reading process can begin.
>
> (Walker, 1975, p. 5)

Walker advocated as essential the need to begin the teaching of reading with isolated skills, for example:

> I am convinced that letters need to be taught very thoroughly before children meet them in words, i.e. before they read.
>
> (ibid. p. 88)

Assessments of 'prereading' ability attempted to isolate skills which in some way related to literacy, but which in themselves were *not* literacy. Teachers in the 1960s and 1970s did not *test* or *measure* early literacy nor did they necessarily view literacy as a socially constructed and holistic process; however, many teachers observed, described and recorded a number of separate literacy and literacy related skills.

Waterland's apprenticeship approach (1985) suggested new ways of observing and recording children's progress in reading. As more schools developed their teaching of reading, often incorporating children's literature into a mixture of reading scheme books, more examples of assessment procedures emerged (Waterland, 1989). In the early 1990s these focused on **recording** rather than **assessing** or **measuring** elements of children's reading. Measures for assessing literacy will be discussed more fully in Chapter 4.

Some adequate measures of aspects of oral language exist (Goswami and Bryant 1990; Frederickson, Frith and Reason, 1997), therefore this book focuses on the need for measurement to support strands of early *literacy* research rather than research into aspects of *oral language* support literacy development. Few, if any, adequate measures of early *literacy* are available. Assessment and measurement should attempt to embrace the complexities of early literacy, therefore the focus on specific strands of early literacy research (environmental print, books and early writing) offers a strong underpinning to assessment of literacy learning in the years when learning is fluid.

It seems that assessment of early literacy development has not kept pace with dynamic changes in teaching, greater understanding of literacy learning, high interest of researchers or changes in government policy. Because children were not considered to have much if any literacy ability before they began compulsory schooling, and because its existence during these early years was largely unacknowledged, there was no apparent need to find ways of measuring children's abilities in this sphere. For a number of reasons – theoretical, political and educational – the problem of early literacy assessment needs to be addressed.

Theoretical reasons for reconsidering assessment of early literacy development

There is now a move from getting children ready to develop literacy skills towards creating opportunities for them to develop their literacy *from the beginning*.

There have been attempts to develop measures of literacy, for use both by researchers who want to carry out specific studies in early literacy, and by teachers in schools who want further to develop their practice. Better measures are certainly needed for researchers engaged in comparative studies, evaluations of interventions, or work on predictors of later literacy attainment. But the development of new measures is not without difficulty. Reporting on a recent evaluation of Reading Recovery in the UK, Sylva and Hurry (1995) stated that

> Measuring reading ability in the lower achievers in this young age group (6;0-6;6) is quite difficult.

> (p. 12)

This assertion points yet again to the need for new and better measures of early literacy development. In the case of researchers, work has tended to concentrate on the development of instruments as an end in themselves or as a method of researching isolated literacy behaviours. For example, Jones and Hendrickson (1970) developed an instrument to measure children's ability to recognise products and book covers and Goodall (1984) developed a measure of four year olds' ability to read environmental print.

Studies considering children's awareness of print (Jones and Hendrickson, 1970) or their knowledge and understanding of print (Goodman and Altwerger, 1981) meant that researchers had to develop instruments with which to measure children's literacy behaviours as part of their research projects. This trend has resulted in a small 'bank' of *ad hoc* measures which are idiosyncratic and not easily transferable to other studies.

Most attempts at such measurement have focused on reading, some have focused on children's recognition of environmental print and there are no apparent published measures of early writing suitable for children under five years. To measure early literacy development a new instrument with a framework which matches current theories of early literacy development is needed.

Political reasons for reconsidering assessment of early literacy development

Methods and purposes of teaching and assessing literacy at the start of the 1990s became subjects of controversy and confusion in the UK, despite the apparent (but short lived) agreement early in the decade between policy, practice and research. Literacy in 1992 was a political issue with claims that reading standards of seven year olds were falling (Cato and Whetton, 1991) and concerns about literacy teaching and achievement continued throughout the decade (Brooks, Foxman and Gorman, 1995). Such claims were linked in some cases to criticism of so-called 'progressive' teaching methods such as the use of children's literature – often referred to as 'real books' – instead of graded reading schemes, and to the alleged lack of teaching children 'phonics' (Turner, 1990) in isolation from the reading context. Others suggested that the apparent fall in reading standards reflected other factors in children's lives, including poverty and a lack of parental involvement (Gorman and Fernandes, 1992). Because teachers' observations of children's work are sometimes not given the status they deserve in assessment, and because such forms of assessment do not always provide necessary research data, there is a pressing need to develop other ways of measuring children's literacy before they are seven years old. Such new measures, based on appreciation of *how* young children tackle literacy as well as *what* they do, might be used accurately to inform the ongoing debate about literacy achievement. Such assessments may point to the need for additional resources in schools where children struggle with literacy and where parents need help with ways of supporting their children's literacy.

Educational reasons for reconsidering assessment of early literacy development

The debate about seven year olds' reading standards seems partly due to the lack of appropriate measures which teachers and researchers could use to assess trends in literacy development. Chittenden and Courtney (1989), in the USA, argued that increased pressures of accountability on teachers of young children made the need for appropriate assessment programmes more acute. They wrote:

> While teachers of young children are expected to view learning to read within the broader context of children's language and development, the standardised tests adopted by many school systems are incompatible with these expectations

(p. 107)

Most of what was available to teachers in Britain in the 1990s relied heavily on individual teachers' judgements as they observed and recorded aspects of literacy. Unfortunately such judgements did not have the status they deserve, but teachers' ongoing assessments based on observation and dialogue have a valuable and essential place as a basis for understanding children's learning which underpins teaching and learning. Teachers' assessments are the best way of diagnosing children's learning needs, but are not the quick 'screening' that is sometimes needed. In the UK, the National Curriculum and its assessment requirements laid down national criteria for the assessment of seven year olds. The setting of National Attainment Targets (and later revisions of these to Level Descriptors) was misguided, and the continued attempts to establish criteria for interpretation and assessment of children's work could not offer standardisation in the administration of related tests to young children at seven years. Standardised conditions did not exist and were not achievable in a system where the organisation of each classroom was decided by the teacher. The statistical concept of 'standardisation' of teaching and learning is arguably, in this context, given more currency than it deserves. Every classroom is different, every teacher is different, every child is different, and the National Assessments were open to teachers' judgements based on their own observations – but not sufficiently open to the additional insights that teachers could bring to provide a fuller picture of each child's literacy. There were deep flaws in this newly imposed system which, in themselves, illustrate the difficulties of devising appropriate assessments of early literacy when there is confusion over purpose. The need for better assessment and fuller recognition of the difficulties of achieving appropriate assessments for different purposes is painfully clear when the development of early Key Stage 1 assessments is recalled.

Developments in nursery education

The need to focus with better understanding on assessment was further highlighted in January 1996 with the publication of the document outlining 'Desirable Outcomes' of nursery education or other 'preschool education' (DFEE/SCAA, 1996a). The document emphasised early literacy, numeracy and the development of personal and social skills. It included a statement of what children should be able to achieve at the end of a period of pre-compulsory education and on entry to compulsory schooling beginning the term after the child's fifth birthday. The statement about language and literacy is clearly about specific achievements of individuals. It must be quoted in full in order to be clear about what aspects of the literacy of four and five year olds mattered to the DFEE and SCAA in 1996:

In small and large groups, children listen attentively and talk about their experiences. They use a growing vocabulary with increasing fluency to express thoughts and convey meaning to the listener. They listen and respond to stories, songs, nursery rhymes and poems. They make up their own stories and take part in role play with confidence.

Children enjoy books and handle them carefully, understanding how they are organised. They know that words and pictures carry meaning and that, in English, print is read from left to right and from top to bottom. They begin to associate sounds with patterns in rhymes, with syllables, and with words and letters. They recognise their own names and some familiar words. They recognise letters of the alphabet by shape and sound. In their writing they use pictures, symbols, familiar words and letters, to communicate meaning, showing awareness of some of the different purposes of writing. They write their names with appropriate use of upper and lower case letters.

(DFEE/SCAA, 1996a, p. 3)

Though *individual achievement* is detailed above, plans for the assessment of these 'outcomes' were confusing. The document stated that judgement would be made not by assessing individual children but:

through inspection, about the extent to which the quality of provision is appropriate to the desirable outcomes in each area of learning, rather than on the achievement of the outcomes themselves by individual children.

(ibid. p. 1)

Given that the above requirements were intended to apply to the whole range of pre-compulsory provision receiving funding through the government's voucher scheme (DFEE, 1996b) it seemed that these objectives would be widely addressed. It followed therefore that some means of individual assessment would be needed eventually even if plans in early 1996 excluded this possibility. This position provided yet more endorsement that early literacy assessment needed to be further examined and developed.

The need for individual assessment was (perhaps inevitably) officially acknowledged in September 1996 (nine months after it was ruled out as a possibility), when the UK government began formal consultation on the 'baseline assessment' of children at five or before, on entry to compulsory schooling. Literacy, along with mathematics, formed the core of proposals for a national framework for the assessment of five year olds (SCAA, 1996a). The draft proposals for baseline assessment issued in September 1996 included performance criteria based upon the earlier document, which described what children should be able to do as a result of some form of preschool education (DFEE/SCAA, 1996a). It set out sample checklists for observations which focused on skills in reading and writing and the document stated as a key principle that a national framework for baseline assessment should: focus as a minimum on early literacy and numeracy (SCAA, 1996, p. 12).

The decision to make baseline assessment a matter of national consultation illustrated political interest in early achievement in general and, more specifically, in the nature of early literacy and outcomes of its assessment.

In 1996, for theoretical, educational and political reasons, the assessment of early literacy was of high interest. The emergence of 'official recognition' of early literacy development in the UK will be examined in Chapter 3.

3

Official Recognition of Early Literacy Development in the UK

This chapter traces key stages in government policy and discusses changes in practice in early literacy education.

Literacy finally earned a place in the nursery education curriculum in the 1980s. Until that time stories were read to children, they looked at books, staff wrote the children's names for them, and nursery rhymes were sung (but often as a 'musical' activity rather than an aid to language and literacy development). Before the age of compulsory schooling children were not generally encouraged to experiment with writing, nor were they expected to show any clear understanding of or interest in literacy. Early literacy development had been overlooked until the late 1970s. In the UK, nursery education showed little recognition of the existence of the literacy abilities of children under five years old, emphasising instead the social and emotional development of children, and concentrating on promoting children's spoken language (Tough, 1976; Taylor, *et al.* 1972; Hannon and James, 1990).

In the 1980s there was a shift in philosophy – from the belief that the 'perils' of literacy learning could wait until compulsory schooling to the conviction that literacy learning begins early and that children before they are three years old could engage meaningfully in literacy activities.

New ways of teaching literacy were developed as researchers and teachers became more aware of *how* children learned about writing and reading. Research and the impact of the National Writing Project, 1985–1989 (initiated by the School Curriculum and Development Committee and taken over by the National Curriculum Council in 1989), also influenced changes in teaching practices. The National Writing Project promoted, among other things: developmental writing, writing for purpose and audience and diversity of written language both in terms of genre and the language itself.

These changes in thinking and practice were given official recognition in 1988 with the first draft proposals for English in the National

Curriculum in which the DES stated that young children were capable of early writing:

> The very youngest children, given the opportunity to use what they know, are able to demonstrate considerable knowledge of the forms and purposes of writing.
>
> (DES, 1988, para 10.12)

In 1988 draft proposals for English in the National Curriculum included in its introductory statements a sense of the developmental nature of early literacy:

> In a child's development listening precedes talking; talking precedes literacy. Each feeds the other and is in turn developed. Children are highly motivated from the earliest stages to respond to the world around them and to communicate their needs; they have expectations, experience pleasure and enjoy success. Witness a baby's reaction to the voice of a parent; a toddler's response to the repetition of a nursery rhyme or the sound of an ice cream bell; the cry of a preschool child of "More, more" when sharing a favourite picture book; the early reading skills of a young child able to select a favourite cereal packet or chocolate bar in a supermarket; the early mark-making of young children given access to pens or crayons; and the vocabulary extension of children engaged in role play as they emulate the actions, language and intonation of their elders.
>
> (ibid. p. 6 para 2.2)

The initial National Curruculum proposals placed some emphasis on reading for meaning and a balance of the 'composition' and 'secretarial' components of writing with programmes of study. There was an underpinning of the importance of relevant and meaningful contexts for reading and writing and the importance of developing writing through play opportunities (DES, 1988, pp. 51–52). Weaknesses of the developing National Curriculum were acknowledged, especially in respect to writing, where the proposals stated that some of the features regarded as most important were not included in writing attainment targets because the proposed new system had no place for them:

> The best writing is vigorous, committed, honest and interesting. We have not included these qualities in our attainment targets because they cannot be mapped on to levels.
>
> (ibid. p. 48 para 10.19)

The Statutory Document *English in the National Curriculum* set out details for Key Stage 1 pupils (5–7 year olds) (DES, 1989b). It maintained the place of what it called 'playwriting' and included the importance of learning writing conventions, and different writing genres. The publication of the HMI report *The Education of Children Under Five* (1989) highlighted the importance of literacy including the use of environmental print, books and stories, opportunities for writing and the development of oral language. The place of play and flexibility in teaching was affirmed as the following excerpt shows:

A nursery school in the south:
The imaginative play area had been organised to provide a hairdresser's shop with improvised hairdryers, a sunbed, and a table with shampoos, combs, brushes, hair clips and wigs. In the shop's reception area there was a desk with a telephone, an appointment book and appointment cards. Throughout the day the children used this area regularly and the telephone booking and appointment area were a centre of particular interest. The appointment book showed clearly the children's emerging writing skills. Written messages contained recognisable letters as well as invented symbols. Much of the interest was related to the exciting variety of writing materials available.

(DES, 1989a, p. 18)

The much acclaimed government report *Starting with Quality* (DES, 1990) also stated the importance of literacy in the nursery curriculum and made a clear statement about children's *prior* knowledge and home learning:

Many (children) will be familiar with favourite stories read to them at home. They will have learned nursery rhymes and TV jingles. Some may be able to recognise their own name in print and be capable of writing it or making marks on paper which closely resemble words. A few children may be capable of reading and writing simple sentences.

(DES, 1990a, part 2 15.33)

A further HMI report published in 1990 used observations of children learning about literacy through play to exemplify good practice in the early years (DES, 1990b).

Three- and four-year-olds in a nursery class were busily engaged in writing letters, addressing envelopes and posting them to other children and adults in the class. In the classroom a post office and a writing area had been set up in connection with a topic on aspects of communication. The children knew that what they were doing in their classroom was an important adult activity in the world outside. They were able to put into practice what they had noticed about letter formation, how English writing moves from left to right, and the structures and shapes of writing. They were able to experience the satisfaction of using writing to draw a response from others.

(DES, 1990b, p. 12)

Following implementation of the National Curriculum at Key Stage 1, Sir

Ron Dearing's review of the National Curriculum and its assessment resulted in proposals to 'streamline' the statutory curriculum (SCAA, 1993). Changes to the English curriculum which influenced Key Stage 1 in terms of emphasis on 'Range, Key Skills, Standard English and Language Study' were outcomes of this review. Though work on literacy learning through environmental print, access to a range of texts and writing through play still remained in the new version of the National Curriculum, the emphasis was shifted to Standard English, grammar and skills (DFE, 1995). This change threatened to widen the divide between what had been learned about how early literacy *develops* and how young children were to be *taught* literacy in school.

The document *Desirable Outcomes of Nursery Education* (DFEE/SCAA, 1996a) detailed what children who had attended voucher-funded pre-compulsory provision should be able to do on entering compulsory education at five years, with emphasis on language, literacy and mathematics.

The 'outcomes' for language and literacy included: listening and responding to stories, songs, nursery rhymes and poems; composing stories, participation in role play; enjoyment and careful handling of books; knowledge of conventions of print; recognition of letters of the alphabet; using writing to communicate meaning; showing awareness of purposes of writing ; and the ability to write their name 'with appropriate use of upper and lower case letters', (DFEE/SCAA, 1996a, p. 3) . This is a far cry from the content and tone of the exemplars of good practice identified by HMI in the earlier part of the decade, where meaning and function were given more prominence than form.

'Desirable Outcomes' demonstrated clearly the intended progression in literacy from pre-compulsory to compulsory education curriculum outcomes, with emphasis on certain literacy skills (DFEE/SCAA, 1996a, p. 10).

Nutbrown (1997) summarises changes in official thinking in terms of curriculum for five year olds, demonstrating the changes in expectation from 1989 to 1996. In 'Reading', for example, in 1989 the lower achieving seven year old was expected to *begin to recognise individual words or letters in familiar contexts* (DES, 1989). In 1995 the requirement for the same group of seven year olds was modified to state that they should *recognise familiar words in simple texts* (DFEE, 1995). In 1996 it was stated that five year olds having attended voucher-funded pre-compulsory provision should, on entry to school, *recognise their own names and some familiar words* (DFEE/SCAA, 1996a). A similar exercise can be done for writing. It appears, then, that expectations are being raised. What was expected of many seven-year-olds in 1989 was, less than ten years later, to be expected of some five-year-olds. Though the documentation is needed for full comparison, consideration of changes as detailed in official documentation raises concerns about increasing expectations of young children in their literacy learning and the possible marginalisation of knowledge of literacy *development* in this process. It is perhaps not surprising then, given the rapid change in stance that led to official recognition of early literacy *development*, that this led to the hasty development of official policy on *assessment* of early literacy development. Proposals were introduced in the latter part of 1996 to introduce a National Framework for Baseline Assessment by September 1998. Literacy was identified as a key element in the government baseline assessment proposals.

Baseline Assessment of early literacy development

There is nothing new about the practice of assessing the achievements of children in the preschool years. The best practice in early years education has always included an element of observing and recording children's learning and progress, sharing these records with parents, and using them as a basis for planning future teaching and learning opportunities. Burgess-Macey, commenting on the 1990s interest in 'baseline assessment', highlighted the change in purpose:

> The current interest in baseline assessment in schools, however, arises from a different source. Schools feel the need to prove that they are teaching children effectively and that the learning that a child can demonstrate by the age of the Key Stage 1 tests of assessment has in fact been facilitated by the school. Without baseline assessment on entry to school the value-added component of a child's later performance cannot be calculated.
>
> (Burgess-Macey, 1994, p. 48)

She stresses concern about purpose and practice:

> Early years educators need to treat the issue of assessment very carefully. We need to be clear about which purposes of assessment we are working towards, and which models of the early years curriculum and of children's learning underpin our models of assessment. We cannot uncritically adopt a model handed down from the National Curriculum and assessment procedures.
>
> (ibid. 1994, p. 48)

Proposals in 1996 (SCAA, 1996a) to create and impose a national framework for baseline assessment carried the potential to restrict early assessment of literacy to the narrow foci as set out in any resulting framework and the risk of restricting innovative teaching practices arising from research findings. For this reason, discussion in this chapter on 'official recognition' of early literacy development must conclude with consideration of government views on its *assessment*. What is worthy of assessment invariably becomes quickly redefined to what is worth teaching, therefore affecting the learning that is valued. Decisions about how to assess hitherto unrecognised literacy development of children before they are five, as they enter compulsory schooling, are fundamental to future debate and decision making about standards, teaching methods and children's achievements.

Before going further there is an important point to be made about centrally imposed terminology. The term 'baseline assessment' is of dubious worth and carries with it a high level of inaccuracy. Though no single term can satisfy all meanings, it seems that 'baseline screening ' more accurately describes the 1997 government proposals and that the term 'entry assessment' is a more appropriate way of describing the beginning of an assessment process undertaken by teachers as part of ongoing school assessment processes. 'Entry' is preferred here to 'baseline' as it implies 'entry' to the school system and does not imply (as does 'baseline') that this particular assessment marks the beginning of learning or of achievement. Important too is the distinction between initial or quick 'screening' and more long term and in depth 'assessment'. This chapter will use the term 'entry assessment' when discussing issues and 'baseline assessment' only when referring directly to government proposals for baseline screening of children on entry to school.

Purposes of entry assessment

To be worthwhile, entry assessment must provide formative and diagnostic information that supports teaching and learning processes. Worthwhile diagnostic entry assessment which informs teaching and learning must be part of **ongoing** assessment practices in schools and help to identify learning needs including special educational needs and particular strengths and interests of individual children. HMI in 1990 suggested that successful assessment and record keeping depended on a number of factors including:

> an agreed policy on the *reasons* for assessing and recording progress: e.g. when is it to be done? by whom? what is it to be for? what are the consequences for children?
>
> (DES, 1990b, p. 29)

As Chapter 4 will demonstrate, clarity of purpose is fundamental to successful assessment. Blatchford and Cline (1992) set out four main reasons for assessment on school entry: a basis for measuring future progress; getting a picture of the new intake; getting a profile of the new entrant, and identifying children who may have difficulties in school. Different assessments are needed for different purposes, and 'entry assessments' designed to inform the teaching and learning of individual children are *not* the same as instruments that are needed for calculation of the 'value added' by a school to a child's learning nor should they be seen as information to hold teachers and schools to account.

> The needs of assessment for accountability on a national scale, and the needs of formative assessment which gives teachers valuable feedback are not compatible – they cannot sensibly draw on the same information
>
> (Barrs, 1990, p. 253)

Efforts put into entry assessment must be in the interests of children and their learning **at the time of the assessment**. To this end assessment processes must be specifically designed for teaching and learning purposes and will provide much information for teachers but may not involve scores that can be used for statistical exercises to calculate how 'effective' a school is in raising achievement. Assessments for other purposes, such as some research projects, 'value-added' calculations or other accountability exercises may require different approaches, with their design providing different ways of recording and scoring outcomes. There are different and sometimes conflicting needs to be reconciled here. There is the clear role of assessment in diagnosing learning needs on which decisions about teaching practices can be based. There is a further role for assessment – the need to demonstrate 'effectiveness' (for example: impact of the school on pupils' achievement, the efficacy of a new initiative in raising achievement, the impact on learning of the style and content of curriculum).

It has also been suggested that 'baseline assessment' results could be used to allocate funding for pupils with special needs. Lorenz (1997) argues that baseline assessment could:

> if it is broad-based enough pick up both those children delayed in their development by social deprivation and those with more class-free disabilities. It should again be an incentive to good schools. With no risk of losing extra help, just when children are beginning to succeed, good schools will be encouraged to use their SEN funding wisely, by making long-term plans.
>
> (p. III)

Lorenz suggests that 'good schools' would have nothing to fear whilst 'poor schools' would have less to 'fritter away'. In putting the case for basing the calculation of funding for pupils with additional needs on baseline assessment and SATs, she asks: 'Why has no one else thought of it?' and concludes 'It's probably just too simple'. Whilst the idea of using assessment as one basis for allocation of additional funding may seem to some to be an obvious purpose for baseline assessment, the task is far from 'simple'. There is nothing simple about baseline assessment. Lorenz (1997) pays no attention to the complexities of baseline assessment and the need to find instruments fit for the purpose. If baseline assessments are not to be used solely for purposes of planning teaching and supporting individual learning, but also to calculate the resources needed for teaching some children, the responsibility of developing appropriate baseline assessment processes comes even more sharply into focus.

Chapter 4 shows a range of measures that currently exist, demonstrates strengths and weaknesses and emphasises the need for clarity of purpose. Few if any single assessment instruments could be claimed to serve the range of assessment purposes. In addition to the availability of a range of appropriate measures there is a further question – who carries out assessments for purposes other than diagnosing learning needs and planning teaching? It is important to ask if it is reasonable – or even ethically defensible – to expect teachers to carrying out screening procedures which do not serve the purposes of teaching and learning.

Collaboration with parents

It is essential that entry assessments provide an opportunity to find out about children's home and prior learning. Individual entry assessment should **begin** with dialogue with parents and they should be enabled (though not required) to participate fully in assessments of their children's learning. The best forms of entry assessment invite parents to contribute and build on home learning. Finding out children's learning needs will help schools to plan appropriate curriculum if the assessment is sufficiently open and not restricted to narrow learning outcomes. Effective teachers begin to understand and respect the learning and thinking of their pupils from the moment they begin school. However, because starting school is an important and complex process for young children, early entry assessments could only be properly carried out if adequate and appropriate classroom support was provided to enable home visiting of families or time for individual assessment work with children new to school. The proposal to impose a National Framework for Baseline Assessment such as that suggested in 1997 carried with it the danger of forcing teachers to focus only on baseline assessment items. This could mean focusing on the things that may well be of least importance to very young children on entry to school, and paying attention instead to externally contrived and narrow learning objectives. This is not the best way for teachers to find out about their new pupils' capabilities. It is not the best way to begin new learning relationships. It is not the first agenda of young children, of their parents, or of their teachers who endeavour to create learning opportunities based on respect for young minds.

Bartholomew and Bruce (1993) expressed their concerns about 'baseline testing and other forms of summative assessment'. In their view:

> Good record-keeping will automatically demonstrate on early meeting what the child *can* do. This is because it is about 'getting to know' the child. A specimen record kept on the first home-visit, or first week in the group, that can be coded for a particular focus is

invaluable as baseline information. Other kinds of baseline 'tests' are probably going to operate in ways that cut across quality in early childhood practice.

(pp. 64–65)

In January 1996 the Secretary of State for Education and Employment asked SCAA to survey current practice on baseline assessment and draft proposals for consultation. SCAA discussion papers for conferences on baseline assessment (SCAA, March 1997a) stated that:

> The Secretary of State in her letter giving the remit to carry out an initial survey and consultation on baseline assessment stressed the vital role that parents play in the education of such young children and asked SCAA to make the consultation of parents a high priority. The existing baseline assessments vary widely in the amount of parental involvement. The input of parents into any form of baseline assessment is felt to be very important by many authorities who feel that parents are able to make a worthwhile contribution to the processes as they know the achievements and interests of their child. Other authorities hold parents evenings to give feedback to the parents about the assessment rather than using the parent as a source of information.

(paper 4)

Participants in consultation conferences were asked if they thought that parents should be asked to give an input into baseline assessment and what part they could play.

Further consultation in September reiterated the importance of 'looking at the role of parents' (SCAA, 1996a). However, a second consultation document in February 1997 made the following recommendations with respect to parents:

> There was widespread agreement with the principle of involving parents/carers at an early stage. There was a general reluctance, however, from those working in schools about additional require-ments. Many made the point that many teachers have had little training in talking with parents/carers and do not find it easy to pass on accurate judgements about children's achievements, particularly if children are achieving below the average for the class.

(SCAA, 1997, para 13)

Despite SCAA's alarming finding that teachers felt ill-equipped to talk to parents about their children's achievements its recommendations failed adequately to address this issue. Instead it was recommended that teachers attend one day of training which would focus on:

> administration of baseline assessment, the use of its outcomes and reporting to parents/carers.

(ibid. para 33)

There is no recommendation that teachers receive fuller professional development to enable them to focus on assessment issues, research and research implications, and purposes of assessment. Given that the 1997 recommendations were that baseline assessment schemes should satisfy purposes of teaching and learning as well as value-added requirements it is alarming that new proposals made no provision for teachers to have opportunities to think about and understand the difficulties of fulfilling both purposes with one assessment instrument.

The focus of assessment

Early literacy and mathematics are important areas of learning for young children and research shows that their home learning can be significant in these areas, but young children are capable of much more than those minimal learning objectives set out in 'Desirable Outcomes' (DFEE/SCAA, 1996a). It would be folly to base a National Framework for Baseline Assessment on these items alone, and risk limiting interest in children's learning to officially stated objectives. Children have much more to tell us about their individual interests and learning in literacy and other aspects of learning – no checklist, profile or test, however carefully constructed, can provide a complete picture of individual achievement in any area of learning.

The range and diversity of entry assessments already developed in many LEAs demonstrate that there is much more to find out about children's learning before school that those items identified in 'Desirable Outcomes'. Narrow and imposed **requirements** for assessment of children's learning, many of whom have not reached their fifth birthday, are wholly inappropriate.

Children need to know what is happening when they are assessed and they are entitled to information about the process which will help them to become informed participants in their assessments. Young children need to be given opportunities to begin self-appraisal, commenting on their achievements and evaluating their own learning. What children think about their own learning is a crucial part of learning itself. If teachers' ongoing assessments are part of continuous teaching and learning processes, their assessments can be unobtrusive as well as open, realistic and informative. Assessment on entry to compulsory schooling should be part of ongoing assessment and assessments should take as long as needed to provide a holistic picture of children's learning, with literacy alongside emotional development as a key part of this picture. In order to do this teachers of four and five year olds need to be supported adequately in their classrooms and in the professional development offered to them.

'Measuring' children's progress

'Measurement' is a complex process and the term implies a level of accuracy which is not always present. Baseline assessment schemes in the government's 1996 draft proposals offered foci for observing, assessing and recording aspects of knowledge but, despite rhetoric about rigour and standardisation, did not provide 'measures'.

Teachers need to be free to use a variety of appropriate ways of finding out about children's learning so that they can usefully develop their teaching and properly support that learning. To require all teachers to use a single, quick, nationally imposed assessment could result in a form of baseline assessment of little use to teaching and learning (its stated primary purpose, SCAA, 1997) and which merely provides data for calculation of 'value-added' or other school accountability. Teachers' assessments should be wholly focused on teaching and learning. To require teachers to spend teaching time providing statistical data that does not support the learning of the children they teach is a highly questionable imposition.

Entry assessments are only useful if they contribute to children's learning. Well developed entry assessment processes can help to monitor children's development and therefore inform future teaching. Such assessments take time and involve reflection, discussion and a willingness to be open to children's learning agendas.

Reporting on national baseline assessments

Whilst it may seem tempting to policy makers to use information collected in the interests of teaching and learning to evaluate progress of five year olds compared across different schools this move would be of dubious worth. Children in their fourth year vary greatly, with many peaks and plateaus of learning and emotion. Because emotions affect learning so profoundly, how children feel cannot be ignored. The reliability and usefulness of a national picture generated from simplistic baseline assessment would be doubtful, and what is worse, using teachers to provide data for national screening could detract from children's learning opportunities.

It is appropriate for schools to consider what they add to children's achievement, and work on school effectiveness takes account of pupil achievement as measured through various assessments. The question at school level is whether the effectiveness of the school should be calculated on the basis of a quick twenty minute screening measure as proposed for a National Framework for Baseline Assessment (SCAA, 1996a), or whether the assessments which teachers use to diagnose pupils' learning needs and to plan teaching could also be used as ways of determining school effectiveness. If entry assessment is to be diagnostic, children's assessments cannot be reduced to a single score. A class summary of single scores is of little use to teachers who must attend to individual learning needs.

Entry assessments must consider all aspects of children's development if they are to contribute positively to teaching and learning. Only entry assessments that are in the interests of children should be introduced, and such assessments should remain confidential between teachers, children and their families.

The assessment of children's literacy on entry to school

Some entry assessments – including those in government proposals (SCAA, 1996a) consider too many important early literacy behaviours en bloc. For example: to know whether a child performs 'in advance of', 'equivalent to' or 'not yet at' the levels identified in 'Desirable Outcomes' is not a useful mechanism to inform teaching and learning. Teachers need to consider more specific literacy concepts, skills, knowledge and under-standing, such as (but not limited to) the detail of knowing about books, children's favourite books, stages of writing development, and knowl-edge of nursery rhymes.

Another proposed scheme included literacy items which corresponded to some extent to what current research has identified as important elements in literacy learning, but again, information that would really contribute to teachers' planning cannot be inferred from a simple check-list. For example – checking off that a child 'knows more than fifteen letters' (why fifteen?, which fifteen?) will not tell the teacher *exactly* what teaching is needed next. A more detailed assessment needs to be done before this item can be ticked off and it is that earlier assessment that is more useful. The information that teachers will obtain as they work with their pupils to fill in this checklist will be more detailed and that assess-ment is the more meaningful. Entry assessments that inform teaching and learning need not be whittled down to this kind of minimal checklist but should contain the detail of (for example) *which* letters children recognise – *that* is the information that enables teachers to plan the next step.

The checklist contained in the government's September 1996 proposals offered no chance to record developing knowledge of writing conventions or understanding of the purpose of writing. Form was emphasised at the expense of 'function', whereas research shows that children learn about the function of literacy first and only later attend with more under-standing to the specific conventions of the form.

Another suggested scheme asked teachers to make open observations of children's learning and interests. This is likely to be the most useful assessment of children; against this rich information the details of check-list scores are rendered unnecessary. Some teachers would need fuller professional development opportunities to consider the wealth of children's learning before five in order to maximise the potential enhancement that observations on entry could offer to quality of teaching and learning. Samples of children's early writing and an observation of their use of books and storytelling would be useful profile items in the entry assessment of children's language and literacy at five.

A report on trials of the three schemes, published in October 1996 (NFER, 1996a), suggested that none of the three was suitable as they stood. It also made the following recommendations:

> From the research findings, it is possible to summarise the characteristics of a scheme that would meet the requirements of most teachers in the study. Such a scheme would:
> * consist of a manageable number of simple criteria
> * cover speaking and listening, reading, writing, mathematics and personal and social development
> * be graded so that the lowest levels of attainment were acknowledged together with the 'desirable outcomes' and higher
> * include a parent conference
> * include an optional descriptive record
> * include guidance on assessing children through the medium of languages other than English
> * include a record of (or at least guidance on) children's language and literacy attainments in languages other than English
> * include discussion of and guidance on the wide range of children's attainments and development to be expected on entry to school
>
> (NFER, October 1996a, Report 1, p. 39)

A further report in December 1996 followed additional trials of assessment items and made further recommendations about the content of items to be assessed. This report set out key items in literacy and other aspects of early development which could be assessed. The report's conclusion is illuminating, as it confirms that there is still much to learn in the assessment of young children:

> These trials have allowed the exploration of a number of hitherto unresearched areas and have allowed initial conclusions to be drawn about several features of young children's attainments and how these may be assessed. In order to continue this development on a sound basis, the materials for optional national use should be based as closely as possible on the findings here. Over the first few years of their use with a national sample, continued systematic research should be carried out to build upon the foundations established here and increase the fund of knowledge in this area of assessment research.
>
> (NFER, December 1996b, p. 101)

This statement suggests that there is much to learn about what is best assessed and what constitutes the 'baseline' in children's early development. Given this, the imposition in 1998 of a national framework for baseline assessment, rather than further exploration and development of the best ways of assessing early achievement, seems premature to say the least.

In January 1997 SCAA's report on the earlier consultation included findings on purpose:

> Nearly all respondents agreed that baseline assessment should provide diagnostic information to assist teachers in planning effectively for children who have just started at primary school. Although the purpose of measuring children's attainment in order to carry out value added analysis generated much discussion, overall there was strong support for it . . . There was some debate about the extent to which purposes for baseline assessment can be met through one assessment instrument. The idea of separating the two purposes and meeting them through two separate sets of activities, possibly carried out at different times, was considered. Most respondents, however, felt that both purposes were about assessing children on entry to school'
>
> (SCAA, January 1997a, p. 2)

'Assessing children on entry to school' is not in itself a purpose of assessment, but part of the *process* of assessment. The *purposes* focus on why assessments are carried out, *processes* cover issues of how and when. SCAA recommended that two purposes – teaching and learning and the value added by the school – should be achieved in one instrument:

> The National Framework should require baseline assessment schemes to provide diagnostic information to enhance children's learning and to measure children's attainment in such a way as to facilitate value-added measures.
>
> (ibid. p. 5)

History will demonstrate the extent to which it proved possible satisfactorily to fulfil both purposes in a single instrument. Present understanding suggests that such a task is more difficult than acknowledged in the above report.

A further report was published in March 1997, which contained material to be submitted to the new Secretary of State for Education and Employment following the election of a Labour government in May 1997. The draft report presented recommendations based on 98 responses from 59 LEAs, 5 teachers' unions and 23 universities, associations and early childhood organisations. This consultation asked about, for example: the clarity of the proposals, the need for amendment to background materials, clarity of criteria for baseline assessment schemes, helpfulness of the commentary. The questionnaire did not give openings for further comment on the appropriateness of *requiring* the assessment of pupils on entry to school (be they just four or nearly five years old). Perhaps this is why some responses indicated disagreement with recommendations already accepted by the previous Secretary of State which included the introduction of a National Framework for Baseline Assessment which *required* that young children were assessed in the way it prescribed (SCAA, 1997a).

An imposed national framework for baseline assessment, based on incomplete research, is not the best option for assessing young children's capabilities and needs as they begin compulsory schooling, and does not provide the best tool for planning effective teaching and enabling progression in learning.

This chapter has documented the official UK position on early literacy and early assessment, beginning with official *recognition* in 1988, and moving rapidly – within a decade – to plans for official *assessment* of early literacy and other aspects of learning to be in place by September 1998.

Chapter 4 considers what currently exists in the measurement of early literacy development as a result of three decades of measuring, assessing and recording such development.

4

Three Decades of Measuring and Assessing Early Literacy Development

This chapter reviews the development of ways of measuring, assessing and recording early literacy development from the early 1970s to the present. It traces trends in 'what counts' as worthy of assessing and changes in expectations of children under five. It shows that, despite three decades of research, there is no adequate measure of literacy that uses *literacy* to assess children. Many earlier tests are flawed because they do not fully *recognise* children's literacy and have attempted to assess what young children know about literacy by considering 'pre-requisites' of literacy (such as colour matching) rather than literacy behaviours themselves (such as using books or writing).

Unlike the range of materials available to assist teachers in their assessment of children's literacy, measures or tests of early literacy development which may be used in research studies which *inform* teachers were in short supply. Table 1 summarises a range of tests of literacy in broadly chronological order to give an historical perspective to the development of work in the field.

Many of the measures listed have been used by some researchers to, for example, evaluate literacy interventions or carry out studies of factors that affect literacy achievement.

It is important to understand the composition of tests and measures used in research (especially) as the use of a test is often taken to add reliability to some research. For this reason this chapter discusses those tests listed in Table 1 in some detail, and in so doing traces the development of literacy tests that many researchers have relied upon since the 1960s.

The beginnings of new measures of early literacy development

In a study of developmental levels of print awareness, Jones and Hendrickson (1970) tested a total of 57 children (26 boys and 31 girls). They were divided evenly into three age groups, three, four and five

Table 1   The development of measures of early literacy development

Instrument	Date	Title/focus
Jones and Hendrickson	1970	Environmental print
Clay	1972	The Diagnostic Survey
Thackray and Thackray	1964	Reading readiness
Downing and Thackray	1976	Reading readiness
Ylisto	1977	Environmental print
Brimer and Raban	1979	Reading readiness
Goodman and Altwerger	1981	Six Literacy Tasks
Clymer and Barratt	1983	Reading readiness
Downing *et al.*	1983	Reading readiness
Heibert	1983	Environmental print
Goodall	1984	Environmental print
Manchester LEA	1988	Literacy
Barrs *et al.*	1989	Primary Language Record
Waterland	1989	Reading
Armstrong	1990	Writing
Sulzby	1990	Writing
Teale	1990	Informal assessment
Kent LEA	1992	Reading
LARR	1993	Reading
Wandsworth	1994	General – includes literacy
Desforges and Lindsey	1995	Infant Index – general includes literacy
SCAA	1996	General – includes literacy
Vincent *et al.*	1996	Literacy Baseline

years, each group comprised nineteen children. The study focused on children's ability to recognise words and images selected from environmental print. The tests involved recognition of two commercial products and two book covers which the researchers were certain were known to the children. Test conditions involved child and tester sitting at a table and the child being shown products and books one at a time. Each time the child was asked a question of the form, 'Do you know what this can is?' Children were shown five examples of the same soup can, each with increasing elements of packaging made more visible. First examples gave blocks of colour only, then some words were added, and eventually the whole can was presented. A similar process was used for book covers. Scoring was numerical with one point for not trying or an inappropriate reply, and two for a correct answer. Credit was given for *how* children got the correct answer, one for using colour, two for using the format, and three for word recognition. The test was designed to assess children's reactions to environmental print in order to establish the extent to which children could 'identify' or 'read' words in the environment. This appears to be the first published measure of early literacy development which used environmental print. Later measures took up Jones and Hendrickson's notion of print recognition.

In a study to test the belief that the onset of reading is not dependent upon phonic instruction, Ylisto (1977) tested 62 Finnish children aged between four and six years old. Children were shown 25 'printed word symbols in the everyday world of a child' (Ylisto, 1977 p. 168). The 25 words used were listed in Ylisto's report (1977) and details of children's total scores are given. Children were tested, interviewed and observed. The test included five stages, listed below, where children were shown print in five different degrees of context and asked 'What does this say ?'

   i.   a photograph of a word in its context, e.g. a label on a door
   ii.   a drawing or representation of the photograph including the word
   iii.   the printed word with less context
   iv.   the printed word with no context
   v.   the written word in a sentence.

Ylisto gave detailed consideration to the skills and knowledge children used to identify the print they were shown and her conclusions relate to implications for the teaching of reading. No conclusions are drawn about the type of measure which was developed to carry out this research.

A more substantial battery of measures was developed by Clay (1972a). Clay's Diagnostic Survey has been developed for use with five, six, and seven year old children. It contains: running reading records; letter identification; 'ready to read' word test; writing samples and writing vocabulary as well as the well known Concepts about Print test. Because this test is still unique and now widely used, particularly in the context of Reading Recovery, it is worth some detailed consideration.

Running reading records were based on Goodman and Burkes' (1972) miscue analysis and taken as the child read using a coding system to indicate errors and corrections. The *letter identification* test consisted of a page of 54 letters comprising upper and lower case including two styles of letters a and g printed in alphabetical sequence from top to bottom and left to right. The child was asked to identify each letter reading across the page so that the letters were not in alphabetical order. The *'ready to read' word test* comprised three lists of words (A, B and C) all identified as the most frequently occuring words in the 'ready to read' series of basic reading texts for young children. The lists were said to be of comparable difficulty. The child is asked to read one of the three lists (chosen by the tester) and performance is scored. The three lists were constructed from material written in the early 1960s.

Instructions on how to score *writing samples* are also included in Clay's Diagnostic Survey. Clay asserts that

> By observing children as they write we can learn a great deal about what they understand about print, and messages in print, and what features of print they are attending to.
>
> (Clay, 1993, p. 57)

Three samples of story writing taken on consecutive days are needed to assess language level, message quality, and directional principle. The *writing vocabulary* element of the Diagnostic Survey consists of asking individual children to write all the words they know in ten minutes. Clay claimed that the test was reliable and had a high relationship with reading words in isolation.

Perhaps the most widely known and used element of Clay's Diagnostic Survey is the *concepts about print* test. This tests 24 'concepts' using one of two test books, written by Clay (*Sand*, 1972b and *Stones*, 1979a). The book is read to the child by the tester who asks specific questions about the text on each page. The books contain aberrations such as upside-down text and misspelled words, which children are required to identify and explain. *Stones* (Clay 1979a) follows similar patterns to *Sand*, but was written later, when Clay in 1979 republished *Early Detection of Reading Difficulties* and included reading recovery procedures for use with children who were identified through the Diagnostic Survey as having specific reading difficulties at six years of age (Clay, 1979b).

Clay suggests that children aged five to seven should learn the 24 concepts listed in the test in the first two years of schooling, therefore five year olds would be expected to score lower than seven year olds. This test gives a possible score of 24, converted to a possible stanine score of 1–9. Average ages at which children should 'pass' each item are given but it is stressed that this depends on curriculum and teaching methods. Apparently straightforward and quick to administer, Clay's *Concepts about Print* test attempted to use book format on a one to one basis to assess which out of 24 items a child knows about print. This battery of instruments was designed to detect reading difficulties early. For Clay the greatest value of this battery of instruments lay in its diagnostic potential. She stressed the importance of observing children's capabilities; solving problems early; matching 'test' tasks to 'learning' tasks of classrooms (rather than standardised tests); and analysis of reading performance (not puzzles or scores). Clay (1972a) stated:

> There is only slight emphasis on scores and quantifying progress – the real value is to uncover what processes and items a particular child controls and what processes and items he could be taught next.

(p. 3)

Whilst the Diagnostic Survey addressed several aspects of children's skill and understanding in reading and their ability to process texts using meaning, structure and visual clues, a major criticism remains. Most of the 24 concepts could be tested with an ordinary book – losing a few items which test children's reaction to printed errors and some opportunities to test children's processing of text using visual clues in the print. The usefulness of this aspect of the test would need to be evaluated in the light of understanding about children's desire to make the texts they read make sense. Children reading for meaning may not respond verbally to some errors because, like experienced adult readers, children who engage with written language make adjustments in order to make sense of the text in the process of reading .

Aspects of the *Concepts about Print* test are within the capability of many four year olds. In the light of what we now understand about young children's literacy it is important to ask why in Clay's sample 'average' children were not expected to be able to identify, for example, 'the front of the book' until they were 5;06 years old. The only behaviour expected of average five year olds was to identify print as different from pictures. A reason for this apparently low expectation could relate to children's previous early literacy experiences or it may simply be due to the expectations teachers had of children in the early 1970s. It is clear that children in the UK at the end of the 1990s are capable of, and are expected to achieve, much more in reading than knowing the front of a book.

Perhaps because Clay's test marked a milestone in attempts to measure early literacy development which matched the way children learned, and perhaps because there has also been no further attempt to develop a battery of measurement tasks such as Clay's, it has attracted other researchers to use it and to publish their comments.

Hartley and Quine (1982) undertook to assess the efficiency of Clay's test with 42 children aged 4;11. They made a number of criticisms about administration. First a difficulty about being 'standardised' as well as 'flexible' was identified, and a second problem was concerned with explanation, when the child is told 'help me to read' and is then questioned on elements appearing on each page. They felt that this could confuse children. In their study, Hartley and Quine found that children tried to search for errors in *meaning* when they were asked to say what was wrong with the page, and they tended to listen, rather than look, when the test required them to look for *printed* errors. The following example may help to illustrate how confusion could arise. In the test book *Sand* (Clay, 1972b) the text reads:

and I splashed with my feet.
I jumped in the hole (*sic.*)

(Clay, 1972b, p. 10)

The tester is instructed to

Read immediately the bottom line first, then the top line. Do NOT point.

(Clay, 1972a, p. 13)

The correct response to this is to say that the sentence should read: *I jumped in the hole and I splashed with my feet*. A child who was reading for meaning might miss the error, as the sentence makes some kind of sense read either way. If the child did not comment on order no score was given for this element of the test. Hartley and Quine questioned the instructions given to the children and expressed concern about such potential confusion. They argued that children may have certain 'concepts' of literacy items which work for them but which they cannot label or yet explain. This is part of the problem of competence and performance. Hartley and Quine end their criticism by summarising seven areas of concern in the following questions:

i. Is the task of supposedly helping the teacher read while actually being tested confusing to the child?

ii. Is the child given enough guidance as to what he is meant to be doing and where he is meant to be looking?

iii. Is the format of the booklet with inverted print and pictures, and jumbled words, confusing?

iv. Does Clay impose a rigidity of questioning and responses which fails to allow the teacher to judge whether a child has acquired a concept? Should the questions allow greater freedom to the child to demonstrate his knowledge and greater freedom to the teacher to evaluate his response?

v. Is Clay testing two areas: namely, concepts that could be acquired before a successful start can be made with reading, and also concepts more likely to be acquired once a mastery of reading is underway?

vi. Has the differentiation between the 'concept' and the 'labelling' term been successfully accomplished?

vii. Do teachers need more guidance on how to help children acquire these essential concepts?

(Hartley and Quine, 1982, p. 112)

Goodman (1981) also responded to Clay's Diagnostic Survey, seeing her main objectives in *Concepts about Print* as:

observing precisely what a child is doing; uncovering the processes a child controls; discovering reading behaviours which need to be taught.

(pp. 445–446)

Goodman considered that Clay's contribution to 'more natural measurement' was significant and that her three objectives are achieved through the test but she recommended that the test should be 'explored' by others in the field, as it provided a basis for discussion. She suggested that it raised questions, provided insights and information of a child's knowledge in an alternative way to 'question and answer' or 'paper and pencil' tests, and was an 'innovative foundation' which should provide a basis for further development of 'natural observation devices'.

Having used the test, Goodman disputed Clay's norms, reliability and validity figures, finding discrepancies between her sample and the scores given by Clay. Goodman suggested that Clay's test was best used for developmental insights to individual children rather than to obtain norm-referenced scores. Throughout her review of *Concepts about Print*,

Goodman stressed 'the greatest value lies in its innovative approach to evaluation'. Suggestions were made about the administration of the test and criticism included the aberrations in print which, like Hartley and Quine, Goodman felt children reading for meaning might ignore. She argued fundamentally with Clay about the use of errors in print, and disagreed about the importance in reading development of overtly noticing certain mis-orders and mis-spellings. Goodman also questioned the cultural relevance of the *Sand* and *Stones* books. If these books, unchanged since they were first produced in two colour printing in the 1970s, are compared with the best of children's publishing in the 1990s it is clear that children are unlikely to be motivated by their appearance or the plot. Despite her criticisms, however, Goodman saw the *Concepts about Print* test as 'a unique contribution to the evaluation of beginning readers' (Goodman, 1981, p. 446), and

> a significant beginning in evaluative measures that provide insight into what children know about written language. It is the first instrument I have seen which uses a real reading experience with very young children to provide information to an observer about the knowledge of how to handle books and of the written language in books.
>
> (p. 447)

These two responses to Clay's test indicate a fundamental problem which needs to be acknowledged and addressed when tests are used to measure literacy development. That is one of viewpoint about how children learn, how learning should be measured and what measurement is for. Clay seemed to focus on assessing a range of skills of *text processing* which eventually came together to make the child a proficient reader. By contrast, Goodman emphasised reading as a holistic behaviour from the start, in which *meaning* seemed to have more emphasis than in Clay's work. Clay's *Concepts about Print* test was intended to identify teaching and learning needs of children who struggled with reading. However, as well as its key role in reading recovery programmes, it has been used in evaluation studies (Sylva and Hurry, 1995) and continues to be used in other research studies which are not related to reading recovery (Neuman, 1996). Given its primary purpose of individual diagnostic assessment to inform teaching, the strengths and weaknesses of Clay's *Concepts about Print* are important.

The criticisms of Hartley and Quine and of Goodman provide useful perspectives from which to begin the 'exploration' which Goodman suggested was needed. Teachers who want to help children who have difficulty in learning to read – the purpose for which Clay's test was designed – could find it helpful and it is indeed used in this way by teachers who work with children on reading recovery programmes. More than twenty years since it was first published, *Concepts about Print* has no apparent successor. The continued popularity and widespread use of *Concepts about Print* shows either how useful it is, or how difficult it is to develop methods of testing and assessing early literacy which match current research. Perhaps both are so.

Measures of early literacy development in the 1980s

Having used and criticised Clay's *Concepts about Print* test , Goodman and Altwerger (1981), almost ten years later, developed a set of 'tasks' which were used to assess different aspects of early literacy development of three, four and five year old children. This work was an attempt to develop strategies for measuring elements of early literacy understanding. Goodman worked from the standpoint that children in a literate society develop the abilities to decode symbols between the ages of two and four years, and that they focus on meaning before they concern themselves with individual letters (Goodman, 1980, pp. 10–11).

As part of a study to explore preschoolers' awareness and responses to environmental print, their attitudes to and concepts of reading and writing and their knowledge and familiarity with print in books, Goodman and Altwerger developed a set of six tasks: three 'print awareness' tasks, two 'concept and attitude' tasks, and the 'book handling knowledge' task. These tasks seem to build on Clay's ideas (1972a).

Three *print awareness tasks* were designed to be presented to children one each week for three weeks. The time interval was needed to administer all the tests to the children in the study and to allow the children space between each task. They increased in difficulty each time as the following details show.

Task 1 Print Awareness
  18 logos selected from household, toys, food and street signs were shown, in context, one at a time to the child.
Task 2 Print Awareness
  A week later the second task uses the same labels with less context (the pictures and other cues removed).
Task 3 Print Awareness
  A week later the words from the same logos used in tasks 1 and 2 were printed in black ink on white card and shown one at a time to the child.

On each occasion the items were shown in a random order and the child was asked what was on the card.

Results given for these tests appeared to show that meaning was important to children (Goodman and Altwerger, 1981). Test three was abandoned for many children as the authors state that children were clearly bored by being asked to simply read words: the previous tasks seemed to have more relevance to the children. Perhaps another explanation was that reading words alone out of context is much more difficult than recognising a logo or word in the context of other colour and graphic clues. Those who watch young children's interactions with everyday print will appreciate children's willingness and abilities to engage with print in a context – where it holds some meaning or message for them.

The final three tasks in Goodman and Altwerger's (1981) set of six were:

Task 4 Concepts of Reading and *Task 5 Concepts of Writing*
These two tasks were administered by individual interviews. In task 4 the child was asked questions which demonstrated his or her knowledge about reading and in task 5 a writing sample was collected.

Task 6 Book Handling Knowledge
This task was adapted from Clay's *Concepts about Print* test and was designed to reveal the child's knowledge and use of print.

These six tasks offered a way of assessing the early literacy development of children age three to five which, though time consuming, was balanced and straightforward. They were a set of literacy tasks which contributed a solution to the problems of measuring children's literacy by asking them to get involved in a range of literacy activities. Particularly useful was the development of the *book handling task*, which built on Clay's work yet used real story books rather than 'test' books and reduced the problems of children misunderstanding instructions which was one criticism of Clay's test. Unfortunately Goodman and Altwerger's work is not widely used by teachers or in research studies as it is more difficult to obtain, whilst Clay's work is readily available.

Tests of reading and reading readiness

In the ten years between Clay's Diagnostic Survey and Goodman and Altwerger's battery of tasks, other tests were developed which focused on different aspects of reading readiness and reading ability.

The *Thackray Reading Readiness Profiles* (Thackray and Thackray, 1974) were developed for use with children of about five years old. Four profiles were devised for testing: vocabulary and concept development; auditory discrimination; visual discrimination, and general ability. They took a total of 70 minutes to administer, a heavy demand for young children. The purpose of these Profiles was to identify areas of 'pre-reading' activity which it was thought would help to *prepare* children to learn to read. In a review of this test Vincent *et al.* (1983) noted some confusion over its usefulness, observing that:

> The profiles are fairly time-consuming in that they require four sessions which will need to be spread over more than one day. Time is also required for the teacher to be thoroughly prepared and

conversant with the contents and exact mode of administration . . .
One useful purpose these Profiles might serve would be to demonstrate to anxious parents clear reasons why a child had not yet
started on a formal reading programme. On the other hand, in no
way should results be used as a reason to neglect the child's development in early reading skills.

(p. 90)

The Thackray reading readiness profiles and Vincent's review illustrate a
view of early literacy that is no longer held by many teachers or by those
who work with teachers to understand more about early literacy development. A further attempt to document children's *readiness for the reading
process* was made by Downing and Thackray (1976) in the *Reading
Readiness Inventory*. The inventory consisted of series of 50 questions
which were mostly to be answered 'yes' or 'no'. Factors relating to four
areas were covered: physiological; environmental; emotional; motivational and personality; and intellectual. This checklist was concerned with
certain factors which might have influenced a child's reading ability but
offer little information about young children's *actual* development in
literacy.

The Infant Reading Test (IRT) developed by Brimer and Raban (1979) is
a measure of word recognition, listening and reading comprehension. It is
a testament to either the robustness of the test, or a further indication of
the lack of research to develop new measures, that this test was still used
by researchers in 1996. Lazo and Pumfrey (1996) reported their use of the
IRT in a study of predictors of what they called *'pre-literate'* children's later
reading and spelling ability. Twenty years after its development few
teachers talk about children being *preliterate* and many would agree that
there are better ways of understanding children's early reading than the
Infant Reading Test.

The 1980s saw a continuing effort to develop ways of measuring early
literacy development, including further work on assessing 'reading readiness' – a concept which had lost currency by the 1990s. Measures of
reading readiness included the Clymer-Barrett Readiness test (CBRT)
(Clymer and Barrett, 1983), a revision of the Clymer Barrett Pre-reading
Battery which was first published in 1967, for use with children aged five
to seven years. 'Readiness' was assessed by teacher ratings of children's
performance on mostly non-literacy abilities: oral language, vocabulary,
listening skills, thinking abilities, social skills, emotional development,
learning attitudes and work habits.

The Linguistic Awareness in Reading Readiness (LARR) Test (Downing
et al., 1983) was developed in British Columbia for use with children aged
4:06–8.00 years. This test, which took up to one hour to administer, was
intended to measure the extent to which children developed understanding of written language. The test was in three parts, recognising

literacy behaviour, understanding literacy functions, and technical language of literacy. In the first part children were shown pictures and asked to identify things which could be read, people writing and writing tools. The second part required children to identify from pictures, people who were using the written word, for example sending or receiving a message. In the final part of the test children had to demonstrate their understanding of the concepts in terms such as 'writing', 'line', 'word', and 'sentence'. A total of 75 items could be tested, with considerable administrative work and preparation.

It is little wonder that long tests which bear little resemblance to the literacy of young children have proved unpopular with teachers and with many who use tests in research studies. Even this brief exploration of published tests shows how out of step many ideas are with what is now known about young children's literacy and explains and justifies some resistance to testing *per se*.

LARR was revised in 1993 to produce a short form for use in the UK (NFER-Nelson, 1993), known as the LARR test of Emergent Literacy. The full title represents something of a paradox: *Linguistic Awareness for Reading Readiness Test of Emergent Literacy*. Since emergent literacy rejects the notion of 'readiness' or 'prerequisites' for literacy the title of this test presents something of a problem – does the test measure 'readiness' or does it measure 'emergent literacy'? As the concept of 'reading readiness' is in opposition to the theoretical basis for 'emergent literacy' both cannot, surely, be measured by the same test?

The 1993 version of LARR has 19 questions preceded by two practice questions. There were two main types of questions in the test: the first group asked children to show that they recognised when reading and writing were taking place and the second group of questions related to pupils' knowledge of terms used in written language. Five of the 19 questions on the LARR could attract up to two marks while the other questions received one mark, the maximum score being 24 points. Further consideration will be given to this test and issues raised by its use in Chapter 7.

The development of measures of early literacy development which attempt to match current ideas about young children's literacy learning

In addition to the measures discussed so far, other researchers were attempting to develop methods of identifying children's ability in literacy which were better matched to their everyday literacy. Heibert (1983) reported an investigation of preschool children's concepts about reading. The study focused on 60 children aged three to five years (20 from each year group), drawn from a predominantly middle class area. It found that a majority of children could identify what reading was; 56 out of the sample of 60 evaluated their own reading ability correctly, and perhaps predictably, five year olds were more able to demonstrate that they knew print was necessary for reading than were three year olds, and four year olds also did better than three year olds on this task. Three tasks, presented individually were used in the study. These were designed to:

i. *assess children's ability to identify reading, both oral and silent:* the child saw an adult reading silently and then aloud and was asked each time what the adult was doing.

ii. *establish children's perceptions of their own reading ability:* children were asked to 'read the secret message' from a page of text. If they said they could read they were asked to do so, if they said they couldn't read the text they were asked if there were other things they could read.

iii. *investigate children's ability to recognise what it was on a page that was read:* children were shown several books with different amounts of print, pictures only, picture and text, text only and blank pages only. Children were asked whether someone who could read would be able to read each book, and if they could, what on the page would they need to look at. A scoring scheme was used to record children's responses to this task.

The purpose of these instruments was to identify preschool children's concepts about reading which could then be used to suggest experiences with which preschool teachers might support children's development. Heibert (1983) suggested that:

Continued investigation of preschool children's print awareness is needed if educators are to design instructional experiences that build on the knowledge that children have as well as to develop appropriate reading experiences for children who come to school having had few experiences with print.

(p. 260)

The instrument goes some way to serve the purpose for which it was designed. However, to be useful in identifying what children know in order to plan teaching strategies and experiences, other aspects of children's literacy, such as book handling and identification of logos, would need to be added. Heibert's tests did, however, *recognise* that something could be learned about what children know about reading by using reading and books. This is an advance on emphasis of colour and shape knowledge and 'reading readiness' approaches.

Other researchers developed measures of literacy development in order to understand children's abilities with environmental print. Goodall (1984) studied 20 children aged between four and five years. Children were shown 22 slides of environmental print in context and later 15 slides were shown with part of the context removed. The study aimed to highlight factors that influenced children's ability to identify print in the environment and whether they used letter knowledge or environmental cues when they appeared to read. This instrument, though specific to the purpose of the study, provided an example of a measurement instrument which incorporated environmental print.

Whilst some researchers focused on environmental print and reading, Sulzby developed a way of observing aspects of writing development. Sulzby's work (1985b) on assessing writing and reading using checklists provides innovative criteria for observation. A checklist of Forms of Writing (p. 94) was used by Sulzby to observe children's writing behaviour in the kindergarten, but few researchers have ways of assessing young children's writing which shows due recognition of their capabilities. Whilst teachers were developing ways of tracking and understanding writing development through 'work saving' the world of some researchers was still puzzling over how writing development could be 'measured'.

Specific assessment instruments for teachers

As schools in the 1980s developed their thinking and practice in the teaching of reading and writing, they developed new ways of assessing children's skills and progress. Waterland (1989) illustrated this with a collection of reading records which were compiled by teachers of young children. All the examples discussed by Waterland featured details of aspects of literacy which teachers could check in various ways as they worked with children.

Some Local Education Authorities responded to the need for different assessment materials and developed language and literacy records which were more in keeping with the increased interest in teaching reading through children's literature rather than only through the use of reading schemes. Still only a few focused with clarity on *writing* of children under the age of five. Records developed by LEAs are intended primarily for use by teachers in classrooms, but some LEA assessments offer ideas which may serve some research purposes.

The Manchester Literacy Record (Manchester LEA, 1988) was developed as part of the Manchester Literacy Project. It suggested formats and criteria for different aspects of early literacy assessment. Profiles of reading and writing were based on observations of children aged three to eight years. These were a guide for the teachers who completed the record sheets, included in the booklet, *A Framework for Assessment*. 'Essential' and 'additional' assessment and recording procedures were given for use at each of the defined stages: nursery (3–4 years), reception (4–5 years), middle infant (6 years) and top infant (7 years). This assessment framework provided teachers with a comprehensive range of assessment processes with formats and techniques including a running record of reading using miscue analysis. Those using this system were involved in ongoing assessment and recording of children's literacy from three to seven years. This aided continuity and progression in early literacy development which are the major purposes behind this set of assessment strategies. The Manchester framework (1988) took young children's developing literacy seriously and offered a way of measuring and assessing it with due respect for the process of learning and assessments as well as for the outcomes.

Perhaps the weakest section of the Manchester Literacy Record is that on parental involvement, although this perhaps reflects the stage at which the project reported. The questions about 'sharing in the literacy assessment' (p. 50) can prompt further discussion around the issues and practicalities of involving parents and they provide an agenda for conversation between teachers and parents, suggesting that the outcomes might be information for parents and a sensitising of parents to literacy learning.

The Primary Language Record (Barrs *et al.*, 1989) set out a system for recording all aspects of language for children throughout the primary age range including those in nurseries. The purposes of this document were explicit. It was based on four principles which stated the purposes of record keeping:

- to inform and guide other teachers who do not know the child
- to inform the head teacher and others in positions of responsibility about the child's work
- to provide parents with information and assessment of the child's progress
- to support and inform the day to day teaching in the classroom.

The record took account of bilingual language development and set out to provide a framework for the teaching of language and literacy.

The Primary Language Record was a 'package' for assessing and recording language and literacy. Inservice training was recommended before it was introduced into a school. It consisted of three parts:

Part A   Space for administrative information and for a record of a discussion between teacher and parents in a 'language and literacy conference'.

Part B   *The Child as a Language User* with sections on talking and listening, reading and writing.

Part C   To be completed at the end of the school year recording comments by parents after seeing the record, a language and literacy conference held with the child and information for the receiving teacher.

Alongside this record was a format for recording dated observations of the child's language and literacy with the following specific headings included in the recording sheet for use when recording samples of reading:

- title of the book
- whether it was known or unknown
- the sampling procedure used (informal, running record, miscue analysis)
- overall impression of the child's reading
- strategies the child used when reading aloud
- child's response to the book
- what the sample showed about the child's development as a reader
- experience and support needed to further development.

Details of all aspects of the record were given in the accompanying hand-book including how to carry out informal reading assessments, running records, and miscue analysis.

Materials developed by Manchester (1988) and ILEA (Barrs *et al.*, 1989) both had multiple elements which employed a range of strategies to assess different kinds of literacy. The result would provide a comprehensive assessment of a child's literacy. Both records involved lengthy tasks and were time consuming for teachers. This has been a particular problem experienced by teachers using the ILEA record, though no published reports state this.

Mitchell (1992) reviewed the Primary Language Record and its suitability for the American school system. She suggested that it 'imperceptibly improves teaching' (p. 150) because teachers are involved in ongoing observation and evaluation of children's language abilities. She wrote:

> The Primary Language record succeeds because it is a team product, it doubles as assessment and as a guide to practice, and it focuses attention on what children can do.
>
> (p. 151)

Barrs and Thomas reported on a validation survey of Reading Scale 1, which formed part of the Primary Language Record. They stated that an early unpublished report in 1986 surveyed 4,000 seven year olds and showed that the scale had 'obvious potential for assessing reading achievement' (Barrs and Thomas, 1991, p. 108).

The development of assessment and measurement in the 1990s

Some LEA material developed in the UK in the early 1990s seemed less comprehensive and more focused on particular areas as detailed in the National Curriculum. The Reading Assessment Profile (Kent LEA, 1992) stated that the materials were designed to:

enable teachers to assess and plot the progress of pupils in the primary years and report to parents with more specific information.

(p. 2)

The materials were presented in the form of checklists, with no space for comments, just the words YES and NO which the teacher was instructed to circle as appropriate. National Curriculum Attainment Targets were boxed, additional reading skills and behaviours were also listed. These materials presented a narrower, if more manageable, format for **recording** but not **assessing** reading. They seemed to be less appropriate to early literacy development than those developed in the 1980s. The profile content was heavily influenced by the National Curriculum, and apparently encouraged 'plotting' reading behaviour on a checklist. This served as an early warning that there could well be cause to worry that assessment of literacy in the 1990s was gradually being narrowed to government set criteria.

Three further examples of baseline assessments, the Infant Index (Desforges and Lindsay, 1995), Wandsworth LEA Baseline Assessment (Wandsworth Borough Council, 1995) and the Literacy Baseline (Vincent, Crumpler and de la Mare, 1996), all published after the introduction of the National Curriculum, provide further indication of a narrowing view of what counts as worthy of assessment in early literacy development, and of increasing compliance with the government view of early literacy. The Infant Index is an example of a standardised baseline screening which includes personal and social development as well as literacy and mathematics. It is in the main a teacher's checklist and though scores have been standardised many items are left to the teacher's judgement and therefore administration may not be comparable from one setting to another. The Infant Index focuses on the following literacy related items:

Reading – (One of the following can be selected to best describe child's ability)
1. Shows an enjoyment of books, and knows how books work – (front/back, left/right, top/bottom)
2. Can recognise individual words or letters in familiar context.
3. Can read from a simple story book
4. None of the above

Writing – (One of the following can be selected to best describe child's ability)
1. Can write own forename (copy writing)
2. Produces isolated written words or phrases to communicate meaning
3. Produces a short piece of written prose
4. None of the above

Spelling – (One of the following can be selected to best describe child's ability)
1. Can discriminate letters from non-letters of letter-like form or numbers

2. Can write some letter shapes in response to speech sounds or letter names
3. Can spell some phonetically regular three-letter words
4. None of the above

The authors continued to evaluate their instrument (Desforges and Lindsay, 1995) and, following feedback from teachers, identified areas where the instrument might further be refined (Sheffield LEA, 1996).

Wandsworth Baseline Assessment (1995) comprises a baseline checklist and the LARR test of Emergent Literacy (NFER, 1993). The checklist items for 'language' include the following literacy items which are directly related to National Curriculum requirements:

*   listens and responds to stories
*   reads pictures and sequences
*   looks at books for pleasure
*   reading
*   names or sounds some letters
*   uses some letter symbols
*   writes own name.

Each of the above items can score 1 (developing competence), 2 (competent) or 3 (above average) on a checklist. Teachers can refer to the handbook of guidance (Wandsworth, 1994) in order to judge at what level the child performs on each item. Strand (1996) reported that these assessments were used by Wandsworth LEA to calculate the value added by the school as well as for teaching and learning purposes. If this is the case, curriculum may well be narrowed down to an assessment that is primarily a tool for the collection of data on school effectiveness.

The Literacy Baseline (Vincent *et al.*, 1996) uses a test booklet which children complete individually, following instructions from the tester. The test, which can be administered in groups of between three and eight children, is designed to be completed in 20 minutes. Items include: phonological awareness – initial sounds and rhymes; literacy concepts – letter names and sounds; reading – pictures to words, words to pictures and sentence to pictures; and spelling. Unfortunately stylised drawings are used throughout and the concepts of 'name of the book' (not title) and 'name of the person who wrote the book' (not author) are tested using a stylised monochrome drawing of the cover of a book. The authors state that the Literacy Baseline is intended for use with children in the first term of their first year of compulsory schooling and that it has three purposes:

*   to provide a 'baseline' from which to measure subsequent progress
*   to contribute to screening procedures designed to identify children likely to face difficulties with the development of early reading skills

- to provide a means of appraising children's early literacy development

(Vincent, Crumpler and de la Mare, 1996, p. 6)

Other than items which test spelling of children's names and six other words (pet, lip, bun, stop, time, funny), children's early writing is not included in this 'literacy baseline'. No account is taken of developmental spelling strategies – each word must be correctly spelled to score.

The government encouraged the trend of development in baseline assessments, and in so doing risked a narrowing of the view of early literacy, with the publication in 1996 of its proposals for a national framework for baseline assessment of all children on entry to compulsory schooling. Literacy items focused attention on National Curriculum literacy, with little value placed on broader literacy knowledge and understanding.

In the UK at the start of the 1990s the National Curriculum set out the content of teaching and learning and corresponding criteria for, and methods of, assessment. The processes and content of assessment in the National Curriculum have caused ongoing controversy, and as the above examples illustrate, have in some cases narrowed literacy assessment to some isolated skills and ignored others which research shows to be important. Armstrong (1990) was critical of this trend and suggested a different way of looking at and assessing children's writing which considers meaning in the evaluation. Taking a single piece of writing by a child of six years, he suggested that children's writing should be considered in several different ways and warns against the use of narrow, nationally set criteria for assessment as this reduces powerful and emotional creative and meaningful writing to a level, a number or a mean score.

Armstrong's treatment of the child's writing gives it respect and worth as a piece of literature. His consideration of this way of assessing children's writing gives further 'criteria' which might be drawn upon if a more holistic approach to the assessment of early literacy development were to be developed. Armstrong argues strongly that children can choose their words carefully and precisely, mixing narrative and illustration to convey power relationships, fear, and anxiety in their writing. He suggests that teachers should view the 'whole' of the writing in order to make a valid assessment, which conveys children's efforts. He argues that elements such as spelling, handwriting and full stops need to be assessed alongside these other attributes which are valued features of literacy as used in novels and play criticisms.

Armstrong suggests that the assessment of writing might consider elements such as: patterns of intention, motifs, orientations, interplay between form and content, technique and expression, and the relationship of the words children write to the pictures they draw. This view of writing leads to a number of questions:

- how do we create a form of assessment which takes account of these things?
- do teachers have sufficient detailed knowledge to be able to do justice to children's writing in this way?
- do teachers have the time it would take to adopt this approach?
- what is the depth of teachers' knowledge about writing?
- do professional development opportunities support teachers in developing *appreciation* of a child's writing in depth?

Whilst there are only a handful of specific assessment tools for early literacy, in the main they concentrate on the assessment of reading abilities and behaviours. Armstrong shows the importance of giving consideration to the assessment of writing as well, although his suggestions apply to children who can follow writing conventions sufficiently to be able to compose their own messages and bring meaning to their writing. Whilst this may be the case for some young children, in the main it is unlikely that children under five would be using writing independently in this way to any great degree and therefore assessments of this quality for preschool children are unlikely. However, there is a message here for those who see young children's writing simply in terms of form, and it is important to recognise that young children learn about genre as they begin to learn about writing.

Sulzby (1990) provides useful definitions of the terminology used in the field of early literacy development, detailing and describing specific items of behaviour. She gives, for example, a detailed list of 'elements':

> scribble, drawing, non-phonetic letter strings, copying of conventional print, invented spelling, producing conventional print, rebus, abbreviation, pseudoletters, idiosyncratic forms
>
> (p. 89)

Which of these elements are noted in assessments of young children's writing?

Useful too is Sulzby's consideration of **timescale**:

> One way of looking at writing development is to consider the 'time of onset' or first appearance of the use of various writing and rewarding forms (Sulzby and Teale, 1985). Time of onset is fairly easy to trace for the forms of writing since the graphic traces are easily observable; children's speech during composition is less well documented.
>
> (ibid. p. 89)

Purposeful assessment instruments could identify some of the graphic traces in children's writing that are described by Sulzby. She considers that some methodological issues of reliability and validity need to be addressed, and reiterates a key problem:

The more naturalistic the assessment, the more difficult it becomes to specify the criteria that observers are using or should be using

(ibid. p. 104)

Sulzby acknowledges methodological difficulties but suggests that commonalities in findings about emergent writing are encouraging, especially as they have been arrived at through diverse methodologies (she cites Ferrerio and Teberosky (1982), Dyson (1984) and Clay (1972a)).

In the final paragraph Sulzby raises a number of valid points about measuring early literacy development.

So what do we have to think about to assess writing by young children who are not yet writing conventionally? We have to be concerned about how close children are to conventional writing and how they are developing toward it. We have to be concerned with the context. We have to worry about the wording we use in assessment. We also need to take into account motivational aspects – Is the child trying ? Is the teacher/assessor encouraging (or discouraging) the child? Writing is a production task, so assessment needs to consider the open-ended nature of the tasks. Writing is variable across contexts, so multiple assessments are crucial. We must keep in mind that we are always assessing the behaviour of one child and thus multiple assessments, while making comparisons with other, usually anonymous, children, have to be related back to this one child.

(ibid. p. 105)

Teale (1990) considers the 'promise and challenge of informal assessment in early literacy' and argues that:

formal tests impose the greatest restrictions on performance since their items tend to be specific and the range of acceptable answers narrow

(Teale, 1990, p. 46)

Teale presents a scale of assessment possibilities represented in terms of a scale/continuum (Figure 1) which shows extremes of assessment from informal observation based assessment to the use of formal tests.

Teale highlights the need for:

research and development that will produce for teachers . . . valid and reliable tools for conducting informal assessment of early reading and writing'

(ibid. p. 47)

Arguing that formal testing of young children is inappropriate, Teale points out that they are inexperienced in test situations (though may have some literacy experience); they are easily distracted; and the tests avail-

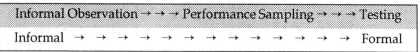

Figure 1 Continuum of Assessment Possibilities

able do not measure 'All the right things' (p. 48). He goes on to suggest that what is measured should be determined by what we know about early literacy:

> becoming literate is a multifaceted process involving attitudes, knowledge, skill, and self-monitoring
>
> (ibid. p. 48)

Because young children acquire literacy skills by being involved first in the activity and the **whole** literacy experience, the kinds of assessments which focus on **parts** do not measure things which 'emergent literacy' emphasises (Teale, 1990, p. 49). Teale refers to several studies of literacy development in home settings to make the point that context is crucial to the assessment. He argues that 'reading readiness' tests do not assess what should be assessed. Conclusions from such tests cannot provide full information about a child's literacy ability, which includes understanding and meaning as well as the technical skills of interpreting written symbols:

> young children's concepts of the functions of literacy are of funda-mental importance to literacy learning
>
> (ibid. p. 50)

He reiterates the problem that somehow our current practices in early literacy development, our present knowledge and children's ways of learning about literacy are not reflected in assessment procedures. Teale states that this is the case in the US (p. 52) and this chapter illustrates that the same applies in the UK.

Teale asserts the best form of assessment. He suggests that informal assessment can be carried out by teachers through observation, collecting children's work, and making performance samples, (p. 53). He ends his paper with four challenges:

i.   more needs to be known about early literacy development
ii. there is currently a paucity of high quality informal measures of early literacy. Large scale efforts must be mounted to develop and field test informal assessment procedures (p. 56)
iii. the quality of informal measures is highly dependent upon teacher knowledge and Teale acknowledges that this necessi-tates vital inservice education and training to support teachers
iv. to be successful in schools informal assessment must be legit-imised and politically acceptable.

Teale concludes:

> It will not be simple but it is certainly possible to bring literacy assessment and literacy instruction together in developmentally appropriate ways

(ibid. p. 58)

Summary of characteristics of existing measures

This chapter illustrates how current measures used for some research purposes do not reflect the literacy which is familiar to children in day to day living. If new measures are to be developed they will need to set the tasks in a meaningful context. To be of use for particular research purposes they will also need to be repeatable and have a scoring system. The content of the measure will need to cover aspects of literacy revealed by key strands of recent early literacy research: environmental print, book knowledge and early writing. If the measure has these features it is likely to be suitable for research involving comparisons (between groups, age spans and methods). Table 2 summarises the instruments reviewed in this chapter in terms of desirable features.

The degree to which the strands of literacy listed in Table 2 are assessed by each of these instruments is not shown in detail in this analysis, which described coverage as either 'adequate' or 'minimal'. Some instruments assess aspects of book knowledge, but only a few use books to do this. This further illustrates the importance of examining instruments for the assessment of early literacy closely and critically.

The summary illustrates that though many instruments have some desirable characteristics, many give minimal attention to some features. Of the measures summarised, three adequately feature environmental print and a further three give minimal attention to environmental print. Five give adequate coverage of book knowledge and a further twelve include reading skills and some book knowledge items but at a level which can only be considered minimal. In terms of writing four give adequate attention and six feature writing at a minimal level.

Three current assessments emerge as the 'best fits' to the characteristics listed in Table 2: *A Diagnostic Survey* (Clay, 1972), *A Framework for Assessment* (Manchester, 1988), and the *Primary Language Record* (Barrs *et al.*, 1989). It is interesting to note that all three have been developed for the purposes of teaching. The latter two are designed for use with all children in the age range, and Clay's *Diagnostic Survey* (1972), though often used in research studies (Sylva and Hurry, 1995; Neuman, 1996), was designed for specific compensatory teaching purposes through the reading recovery programme (Clay, 1979b).

Table 2   Summary instruments reviewed in this chapter in terms of some desired characteristics of a new measure of early literacy

Test	Sets tasks in meaningful context	Covers knowledge of environmental print	Covers knowledge of books	Covers writing	Can be repeated	Has a scoring system
Jones and Hendrickson 1970	–	✓	–	–	?	–
Clay 1972	–	–	✓	✓	✓	✓
Thackray & Thackray 1974	–	–	•	–	?	–
Downing & Thackray 1976	–	–	•	–	?	–
Ylisto 1977	✓	✓	–	–	?	–
Brimer & Raban 1979	–	–	•	–	?	✓
Goodman & Altwerger 1981	–	•	•	•	✓	–
Downing *et al.* 1983	–	•	•	•	✓	✓
Clymer & Barratt 1983	✓	–	•	–	?	✓
Heibert 1983	✓	–	✓	–	?	–
Goodhall 1984	✓	✓	–	–	✓	–
Manchester 1988	✓	–	✓	✓	✓	✓
Barrs *et al.* 1989	✓	–	✓	✓	✓	–
Waterland 1989	✓	–	✓	–	✓	–
Sulzby 1990	✓	–	–	✓	✓	✓
Kent LEA 1992	–	–	•	–	✓	✓
LARR 1993	–	•	•	–	✓	✓
Wandsworth 1994	✓	–	•	•	✓	✓
Desforges and Lyndsay 1995	✓	–	•	•	✓	✓
SCAA 1996	✓	–	•	•	✓	✓
Vincent *et al.*	–	–	•	•	✓	✓

Key:
✓   adequate coverage
•   minimal coverage

Some remaining issues

This chapter has examined some ways of assessing the literacy development of young children, and given a picture of the evolution of early literacy assessment and the present situation. The considerable lack of available measurement tools in the field is highlighted and leads to four areas of concern which will be discussed in turn:

- Many existing ways of assessing preschool literacy development are out of step with what is now known about how children acquire their literacy.
- The measurement of early literacy development is in its early stages.

- Culturally transferable tests are difficult to develop.
- New measures are needed.

Many existing ways of assessing preschool literacy development are out of step with what is now known about how children acquire their literacy.

Goodman and Altwerger (1981) wrote:

> evaluation of reading development based on knowledge of print in books alone is inadequate to gain insight about what children know about print in all environments
>
> (p. 27)

Most tests and assessments de-contextualise small elements of literacy for the purpose of assessment. Tests may focus on a range of skills such as, letter recognition, knowledge of letter sounds, ability to match letters and sounds. Few tests provide a means of assessing or measuring children's literacy development which takes account of literacy and all its complexities. Children's reading and writing ability often depends on their understanding of the purpose and audience and the contexts in which they find themselves. Given the importance of context to the process of literacy learning, it could be argued that tests which disregard context and focus only on small elements of behaviour which are part of reading or writing processes might therefore be invalid as tests of literacy.

The 'measurement' of early literacy development is in its early stages

Despite three decades of research and development involving assessment of literacy skills, the fact that researchers are developing test material as and when they need it for specific research projects shows that a need continues to exist for naturalistic means of measuring early literacy development:

> No standardised reading readiness test we know of measures children's attitudes or concepts of reading, their knowledge of environmental print or their experience with books.
>
> (Goodman and Altwerger, 1981, p. 31)

Teale (1990) argued that formal testing of early literacy development is inappropriate, while Sulzby offers some help in deciding what informal assessment might include. She points out that different researchers, using a range of methodologies, have now contributed to a resource bank of information about how young children develop their early literacy behaviour and understanding. This, argues Sulzby, gives validity to the claims about early and emergent literacy, and she suggests that we move from what we know about literacy to develop assessment tools based on the same knowledge. Sulzby's position is that such assessment tools would be equally valid because they are derived from a valid base.

There is support for the notion that, for some research purposes, the measurement of early literacy development would benefit from the development of a holistic approach with instruments which take account of the multifaceted nature of literacy itself. Batteries of tests, or tasks, that draw on the kinds of tasks teachers would work on with children in everyday teaching, learning and assessment contexts, would probably be most useful if comprehensive detail is to be obtained about a child's literacy, but questions remain. How is this to be done? How long would it take to assess each child's literacy?

Though professional development opportunities on assessment are few, support materials for teachers are abundant. Many Local Education Authorities have produced assessment material for early years, literacy being part of a whole curriculum approach to assessment. Less material is available for researchers who, for particular studies, may seek ways of measuring early literacy development of children aged three to five years, as part of experimental or case study work. This problem needs to be pursued because if teachers are to draw on the outcomes of these studies, the measures employed must have credibility. It is no longer acceptable for researchers to justify using tests of literacy by claiming that they were selected because they are 'widely used' or they are 'standardised'. Popularity, availability and standardisation alone are a poor rationale for the selection of measures of literacy. What the test looks like – whether it looks as if it focuses on appropriate elements of literacy – is another test of validity that needs to be applied.

Culturally transferable tests are difficult to develop

Clay (1972a) and Goodman and Altwerger (1981) came nearest to a balanced set of measures for early literacy development. They are both different: Clay's material gives the impression of being transferable from one national context to another, yet it is less 'natural', whilst Goodman and Altwerger's Print Awareness Tasks cannot be so directly transferred to other countries and contexts, and is difficult to obtain.

For any assessment of environmental print awareness to be useful in the UK, Europe, or the wider world it would have to include a different set of logos. The development of such a measure would need to see a way of *selecting* logos as a more important factor than the specific logos used. Only in this way could the assessment be adopted in different countries and have some chance of being culturally appropriate, with reduced bias, and 'fair' (i.e. appropriate to children living in the area). Even within the UK, taking only English words, there is a risk of cultural bias amongst children who speak English as a first language or who live in different parts of the same country. For children who speak English as an additional language the selection of environmental print examples is a crucial factor.

The system of selection is therefore much more important, in terms of transferability, than the final list of print used. To be used at intervals, logos may need to change so that there is continued relevance and they should therefore be selected according to the same criteria as the initial set.

New measures are needed

In terms of the characteristics of measures summarised in Table 2 there appears currently to be no instrument which :

- is suitable for research requiring comparisons (between groups, age spans and experiences)
- covers the three to five year age range
- covers aspects of literacy revealed by key strands of recent early literacy research: environmental print, books and early writing
- can be repeated
- has a scoring system.

New measures with these characteristics need to be developed.

This chapter examined a number of measures of literacy which attempt to assess aspects of early literacy; Chapter 5 will draw on this review to examine the purposes of assessing literacy.

5

The Purposes of Assessing
Early Literacy Development

This chapter considers various purposes of measuring and assessing children's early literacy development. Decisions about how best to assess children's abilities will depend on the reasons for that assessment. Different groups of people, with varying interests in children's literacy development, require different measures. Their choice of measurement techniques will depend on their reasons for assessment and the purpose for which they intend to use the outcomes. The way outcomes of assessment are presented also reflects purpose, for example, if results are to be used to compare groups of children, performance of schools, LEAs, and so on, then statistical information will be required. Teachers, however, are essentially interested in diagnosis of individual learning and development and therefore details of children's knowledge and understanding are of much more value to them than a single, final score. One could argue that teachers do not need numerical outcomes at all, because their job is to make a difference to the learning of each individual in their class – scores alone do not help them in this task. Some methods of assessing and assessment instruments outlined in Chapter 4 are examined here in terms of their fitness for purpose.

There are questions to be asked:

1. Who assesses children's early literacy development?
2. Who is concerned with assessment results?
3. Why should early literacy development be assessed?
4. Which purposes are served by existing instruments?
5. Which purposes might be better fulfilled?

Who assesses children's early literacy development?

In UK schools a number of different groups carry out some form of assessment of preschool children's literacy development. They include:

nursery/class teachers, special needs teachers, headteachers, parents, psychologists and researchers.

- **Nursery/class teachers** carry out formal and informal assessments as part of the teaching and learning process, to aid planning and also as a legal requirement at the end of Key Stage 1 in the National Curriculum and, from 1988, as a legal requirement to assess children aged four or five years on entry to school. Formal testing was also introduced in 1996 where some schools became part of the first cohort of schools working with the newly established 'Literacy Centres' in the National Literacy Project.
- **Special needs teachers** use diagnostic assessments in order to decide on necessary teaching and later to ascertain the effectiveness of that teaching.
- **Headteachers** sometimes administer reading tests, including reading assessment tasks for National Curriculum end of Key Stage 1 assessment.
- **Parents** assess their children's performance informally, though rarely formally. Their assessments are ongoing, they may compare their child's abilities with those of other children, checking what they can do and what they know. Some parents are also invited to participate in assessments carried out by teachers.
- **Psychologists** carry out diagnostic assessments of children who are considered to have particular needs. It is not uncommon for psychologists to make use of more formal tests.
- **Researchers** engaged in particular kinds of evaluation need to carry out assessments.These may take place at the start of research projects and throughout projects.

With this diversity of assessors, purposes clearly vary. Teale (1990) considers assessment to be 'a process of gathering data and using those data to make decisions' (p. 45).

The range of people and interested groups involved in carrying out assessments leads to a consideration of the greater diversity amongst those interested in the *outcomes* of assessment and the nature of decision making which ensues.

Who is concerned with assessment results?

In addition to the groups already mentioned, there seem to be two other main groups interested in the outcomes of early literacy development assessment: Local Education Authorities and politicians (particularly the government of the day). In both cases children's assessment results could be used as forms of accountability. In the case of politicians, assessment outcomes may be used to illustrate the effectiveness of certain political initiatives or a justification for government decisions. As the publication in March 1997 of 'league tables' of end of Key Stage 2 results illustrated, test results of older children have been used in the debate about standards of literacy, and also in wider political issues such as teaching methods, or the politics of Local Education Authorities. Assessments which are of practical use to teachers and informative for parents are less likely to provide the statistical information required by politicians. Information for political debate or for decision making is often required in the form of statistical evidence. This leads us to a deeper consideration of purpose and begs the question of *why* early literacy development should be assessed.

Why should early literacy development be assessed?

Appropriate ways of assessing children's literacy development are needed for work in three broad areas: teaching, research and policy.

Assessment for teaching

Methods include: charting development, monitoring progress, saving examples of work, talking with children, talking with parents, making observations, diagnostic screening instruments and fuller formal diagnostic assessment instruments.

Teachers need effective assessment tools which reflect teaching methods and support teaching and learning. They currently have few adequate quantitative means of defending or advocating their practice and it is arguable that this is not their role – and formal testing may not give them more or better insights into the learning of the children they teach. Gardner (1986) suggested that:

> formal testing of reading is unlikely to be more reliable than some form of teacher judgement . . . observing the response of individual pupils to a variety of reading assignments over a period of time provides the essential information from which an assessment of progress and ability can be made.
>
> (p. 67)

The kind of assessment advocated by Gardner may provide valuable information for teachers to make decisions about teaching and learning needs, as can the 'First Steps' approach which links curriculum planning with individual assessment (Education Department Western Australia, 1994, 1994a). Such assessment does not provide the statistical data required by some to inform the debate about standards but it does help teachers to base their teaching on the individual learning needs and literacy abilities of the children they teach.

Assessment for research

Current pressure to raise standards in primary education means pressure for teachers. At present there is no means of knowing whether teachers, teaching methods, resources, parental involvement, or outside factors such as family poverty are in part or in whole responsible for levels of children's reading ability. Neither does there exist any reliable way of determining trends in young children's reading ability.

It is not appropriate for teachers to be burdened with extra testing and measuring of children's literacy ability in order to satisfy political and policy pressures, but there is a key role here for research.

Measures in this category include:

i.   instruments used to evaluate:
  * research programmes
  * intervention studies
  * teaching methods and content (including National Curriculum)
ii.   instruments which could identify trends in literacy acquisition making it possible to understand relationships between different factors, for example: gender and literacy; literacy and poverty; teaching, learning and achievement, predictors of literacy achievement.

Assessment for policy makers

Policy makers in the UK at the end of the twentieth century require statistical evidence of trends in literacy standards. Such figures might then be used to provide the public with information which make political points – local and national 'league tables' of school performance which are then used to judge school and LEA performance are examples of such use. Assessments used for this purpose in the UK are devised centrally and administered by teachers as a legal requirement. For policy makers who control what is devised and imposed nationally the theoretical credibility of measures may not be a major concern. More important may be the way in which assessment results serve a political desire to demonstrate 'failures' or 'successes'.

What must be clearly understood by policy makers and other interested parties is that assessment which makes a difference to teaching and learning is not the same kind of assessment that provides quickly gathered data and numerical outcomes.

Which purposes are served by existing instruments?

Of the three main purposes for assessment – teaching, research and policy – some seem better served by exisiting instruments than others. Chapter 2 suggests that a number of assessment processes exist for teaching purposes (for example: Manchester, 1988; Barrs *et al.*, 1989; Clay, 1972a).

Whitehead (1990) argues that education and testing are different and separate activities:

> we and the children must be clear that these test exercises are separate from the real business of learning and doing in the early years classrooms. Playing the testing game must be organised in ways that produce the statistics while protecting the young learners from the stresses of competition and early failure. The activities of education and testing are different, they have different purposes and involve very different processes.
>
> (p. 93)

Teale advocates that systematic observation and performance sampling are the most appropriate means of assessing young children 'to obtain information that promotes good literacy instruction'.

Teale's suggestions (1990, p. 53) are encouraged in the UK with support materials and assessment packages available for teachers to use to assess children's literacy. They are not without flaws. There are no perfect offerings in the world of literacy assessment. Teachers are urged to encourage vigorous and committed writing, yet such qualities are not often considered in terms of assessment. Armstrong (1990) is critical of the neglect of meaning in the National Curriculum. He quotes from the first report of the National Curriculum English Working Group which stated:

> The best writing is vigorous, committed, honest and interesting. We have not included these qualities in our attainment targets because they cannot be mapped onto levels.
>
> (DES, 1988, para 10.19, p. 48)

Meaning is also considered a crucial factor by HMI:

> Some of the best writing was a direct and sincere response to personal experience.
>
> (DES, 1990b, p. 5)

The National Writing Project found that children did not see meaningful writing as a priority in assessing its quality:

> Often the superficial features of writing – neatness, presentation, correct spelling – were considered to be most important, and were used by children to assess whether writing was good and whether the writer was successful.
>
> (National Writing Project, 1989, p. 17)

Teachers carrying out informal assessment of early literacy development, rather than more formal testing, are more 'in tune' with current theoretical understanding in the UK and the USA of how young children *develop* their literacy. Chittenden and Courtney (1989) suggested ways of 'documenting' children's literacy development, following uniform criteria but allowing for flexibility according to development and performance. They rightly argued that this was a more appropriate way of generating detailed information about children's progress in literacy development than testing.

Which purposes might be better fulfilled?

For some kinds of research into early literacy development, few, if any, appropriate measures exist. There is little which can be used for evaluation either of teaching programmes (including National Curriculum), curriculum initiatives, or other interventions. The use of measures is often justified on the basis that such measures are widely used (presumably because little else exists) or that they are standardised (Riley, 1996). Neither are good enough reasons for occupying children's time with the activities they involve or perhaps for building research projects upon then. Valid measurement for the purposes of research can be different from the forms of assessment teachers use. Assessments for particular kinds of evaluative research can require a different kind of accountability, a different set of criteria and different level of detail. Where children's literacy development is measured as part of a research initiative, issues of standardisation, validity and reliability may also need to be resolved. Measures often need to be carried out in a short space of time. Because of this, the types of assessment procedures used by teachers who observe and assess their pupils over a period of time, and through daily interaction with them, cannot be used easily by researchers who require a brief measure at various ages. Present measures of preschool literacy needed for the research purposes listed earlier (page 75) do not reflect current understanding about early literacy development in which researchers are now increasingly interested.

Sulzby (1990) points to this problem when she states:

> The status of research on the assessment in young children's writing currently is **thriving** but only just **beginning**.
>
> (p. 85)

As research extends the knowledge base of early literacy development, so approaches to assessing and measuring literacy need to change to take account of this. Morrow and Smith (1990) are clear about the place of assessment and measurement in education:

> Assessment and measurement should match educational goals and practice. Many early literacy researchers argue that traditional standardised tests do not reflect the practice that has evolved from the new theories based on research. In addition, standardised tests are only one form of measurement; we have come to realise that these alone are not adequate assessments of total literacy development.
>
> (pp. 3–4)

Perhaps measures for some research purposes need to be informal in their administration, but formalised in their construction and analysis. Credible research can depend upon appropriate measures. Assessments which rely upon observations of children using literacy do not always fully satisfy these criteria. There have been some attempts to develop assessments which draw upon current research into children's literacy (Goodman and Altwerger, 1981; Goodall, 1984; Jones and Hendrickson, 1970) but these can present some problems. Such tests as these need to be more reliable, with a clear method for selecting test books and logos and criteria for presenting the logos in grades of difficulty to children. Scoring needs to be developed and ways need to be found of interpreting the data and relating them to literacy behaviours. In all of these processes, the integrity of the assessment instrument will depend upon ways in which the instrument reflects what is known about how young children learn and what literacy they meaningfully engage in, and whether the instrument, its administration and outcomes are matters which retain respect for the children who are being assessed. In the late 1990s and the early 2000s research involving measurement of early literacy should cast off the legacy of psychometrically designed tests which are divorced from the realities of literacy development. In their place should be measures more closely linked to the literacy of children's everyday lives. This is a tall order. The task is to develop a range of measures which allow some statistical analysis, but which are based on knowledge of developmental literacy and which maintain the authenticity of literacy within the measure.

Problems of assessment of reading of seven year olds in the UK were apparent in the development of a national testing programme in the early 1990s. The procedures were rewritten after the first year and continue to be revised. Problems included massive administration work for teachers, time consuming activities and unresolved issues of standardisation. We have yet to see the extent to which such problems also beset the national framework for baseline assessment to be imposed in 1998.

If research can begin successfully to address the issue of measurement of early literacy development, this may have an effect on the information which then becomes available through research to policy makers. Ultimately this could result in changes in policy which lead to more appropriate assessment and better use of assessment outcomes.

6

Purpose and Practice in
Early Literacy Development

Clarity of purpose, as Chapter 5 has argued, is essential to decisions about which types of assessment to use. This chapter takes the issue of purpose and explores the relationship between purpose and practice. Drawing on a detailed survey of 30 schools with nursery or reception classes in one LEA, three themes are addressed:

- assessment for teaching
- the impact of policy
- teachers' assessment needs.

The first is given more attention because it lies at the heart of teachers' practice. The remaining two themes are discussed in terms of their impact on assessment for teaching.

Chapter 4 showed that a range of assessment procedures were available for teachers to use with young children and Chapter 5 discussed purposes of assessing early literacy development. These chapters lead to the conclusion that teachers already have the tools available to carry out holistic assessments of early literacy development over a period of time using mainly observation and reflection.

Teachers' reflections on their purposes for assessing are important, so this chapter presents the views of over 30 teachers who, in the early 1990s, were asked to think about their assessment practice, and reflect on the issues which surrounded their assessment of young children's literacy.

Thirty schools (25%) from one LEA in the UK were chosen to participate in the survey carried out during the period from September 1991 to February 1992, at the dawn of National Curriculum assessment at Key Stage 1. Two criteria were applied:

i.   children age five and under attended the schools
ii. a range of socio-economic areas were represented.

Sampling was designed so that three distinct groups of schools were targeted to cover the bands of age range shown in Table 3.

Table 3 Age bands, age ranges, numbers of schools, and proportions in the survey sample

Age band	Age range	Number of schools	Proportion of schools in the survey
A	'under fives' only	5	16.5%
B	'fives and over'	5	76.5%
C	'Under fives' and 'fives and over'	20	17%

This division of types of school and their age ranges represented reflected the proportion of these types of schools in the LEA where the survey took place.

A total of 37 teachers were interviewed. All interviews were held with a person with some responsibility for decision making, generally the head teacher or the teacher responsible for language, assessment or the nursery. In seven cases two people offered to be interviewed. The numbers were as follows:

18 head teachers
14 nursery teachers
2 language co-ordinators
2 deputy head teachers
1 infant co-ordinator

The interviews were arranged with the agreement of the head teacher and advisers and officers in the LEA. Each interview followed a similar pattern. In 20 of the 30 schools, examples of record-keeping documentation were also collected. The following questions formed the basis of each interview:

Question 1 *Do you have any records for early literacy development or bits of reading and writing development? If so, can I see them, take copies? If not, how do you keep a record of children's early literacy development – e.g. saving work, tests, teachers notes?*
Look at records together if possible and note how the record works and who contributes and when (how often) it is done. *Do you feel this record serves your purposes?*

Question 2 *Do parents contribute to record keeping of early literacy?*

Question 3 *Do children play any part in their own assessment? For example, do they make comments about what they like or can do?*

Question 4 *Is literacy the only subject based record you have or are there similar records for other subjects (for this age group). If so why . . . what?*

Question 5 *How do your literacy records fit with National Curriculum Assessment? Have you developed your current records for literacy since the National Curriculum Assessment?*

Question 6 *What would you say are the main purposes of literacy record*

keeping and assessment at this time of children's development?

Question 7   What would you really like to help you with recording literacy and its assessment? What would really help?

Question 8   Is there anything else about literacy, assessment and record keeping which you think is important?

Main findings from survey

Most important here are the teachers' views. The main findings from the survey can be discussed under the following themes:

- assessment for teaching
- the impact of policy
- teachers' assessment needs.

In the following discussion the comments of teachers are at the forefront.

Assessment for teaching

A number of points relating to assessment as part of the practice of teaching were raised. These are discussed here in terms of four broad areas: continuity and progression, parental involvement, record keeping and assessment, and teachers' purposes for assessing and recording.

Continuity and progression

The 25 nursery schools and classes which participated in the study all had record keeping systems specific to the age group of the children they taught. All the nursery classes had record keeping systems which were on the whole separate from those used in the school to which they were attached.

Ten nursery teachers saw records as a way of ensuring continuity of learning experiences between nursery and reception classes.

> I hesitate to say passing it on, but it is important. Passing on to other adults working with children so they are aware of what they can do – continuity of learning and experience.
>
> Nursery teacher

> For passing on to other teachers – they're not starting with a blank slate. Not all these four year olds will need to learn initial sounds, some know them, learned them at home! So I can tell the reception teacher that.
>
> Nursery teacher

> Our new records fit well with programmes of study so they are really useful for transition into school. Teachers in school like to know what they can do.
>
> Nursery teacher

The literacy record goes from reception to eight years. This next year we will start it in the nursery, but one or two details will need to be added to take account of the literacy development of very young children.

Head teacher 3–8

We have seen children who are really into writing now – I think it will be important to send examples of this through into school so that their teachers can see what they've done so far.

Nursery teacher

There was one case where the separation between nursery and school meant that there was little communication about records:

I've never seen the school records. I've no idea what records other than achievement folders and attainment targets they have.

Nursery teacher

The use of achievement folders which involved saving examples of children's work, teachers' observations, and comments from teachers, children and parents was a way of providing some continuity from nursery to school and eight of the 20 nursery classes had some form of achievement folder established.

We keep track of writing development through work saving as part of achievement folders

Head teacher 5–7

Achievement records begin in nursery and continues through school.

Nursery teacher

Work saving including quite an amount of written work is part of each child's record file.

Head teacher 5–11

Nursery has taken the lead in individual achievement records, started it off and sustained involvement throughout the school.

Nursery teacher

In a small number of cases where individual achievement records was a 'whole school' initiative the nursery had not been involved.

I don't know why we don't start with achievement records in the nursery (it runs through the rest of the school).

Deputy head teacher 3–11

Parental involvement

Nine schools said that they involved parents in recording children's literacy development. In six schools parents of children aged five and over made written comments in children's personal reading note books after listening to them read at home. Teachers also commented in these books, recording their observations of children's reading in school.

They are useful for informing parents.

Nursery teacher

For parents to contribute to children's learning and development.

Nursery teacher

It's for parents – so you can say 'look how she's getting on with this'.

Nursery teacher

There is a space for parents to comment on the record. They can see it termly, or perhaps just once – it depends.

Nursery teacher

In one case there was a strong feeling that professional trust of the teacher by parents meant that sharing records was neither appropriate nor necessary.

Parents trust us – they trust the teachers to teach them – it's like me trusting a surgeon if I need an operation. They don't need us to account to them, they see us as the people who have the skills to teach their children and let us do it, it's about trust.

Head teacher 3–8

A further three schools involved parents of children aged three to five years in commenting on and recording aspects of their children's literacy development, saying things like:

We have found some ideas for records that staff could use with parents.

Nursery teacher

I'd like to be able to draw more on what parents say.

Nursery teacher

We give our record to parents and explain how different bits fit together. We ask parents to fill this in and return to us. Then nursery staff fill in things they've noticed too, then it goes home again – it goes backwards and forwards during their time in nursery.

Nursery teacher

Record keeping and assessment tools

Not surprisingly, the survey found no examples of teachers of three to five year old children using formal assessment or measurement procedures related to children's literacy. All the work carried out focused on observations, saving examples of children's drawing and early writing, and making written records based on this type of evidence. Teachers seemed content that this was adequate for the age of children they worked with, and some had actively developed different formats for recording development.

i. Procedures and processes

Some teachers highlighted the importance of observing and recording in detail aspects of children's literacy development:

> Two language support teachers developed a record for bi-lingualism . . . Bilingual records for reading, speaking, listening and writing were developed since the National Curriculum. They are all into observation, record keeping and emergent literacy, but it is having time to share all that adequately.
>
> Nursery teacher

> We record separately in reception year because there are so many little steps of development. In the rest of school we record language and literacy on a sequential development ladder using teachers' observations.
>
> Head teacher 5–7

> For literacy there's too much – it's too broad – so saving work gives a more whole approach.
>
> Infant co-ordinator 3–11

In one case the school felt that literacy was important, but other pressures had meant that they could only acknowledge that it was important to develop and assess it in the early years:

> It is awful to say but I can only say we're thinking about it. I know that the National Curriculum Attainment targets are inadequate for recording children's literacy development but at the moment we have nothing else.
>
> Deputy head teacher 3–11

This comment perhaps reflected the pressure that new national assessments of seven year olds caused in the early 1990s. It is a warning that imposed assessment procedures can have the effect of narrowing what is assessed. There lies here a danger of limiting what is taught and learned.

ii. Philosophy – the need to record literacy

There were varying responses which related to thinking about the importance of recording early literacy development. A very few teachers felt it was not necessary to record any aspects of early literacy:

For the moment we don't record it [literacy development], it's obvious, so we don't really need to write it down.

Nursery teacher

Other teachers felt that it was important to record literacy development in detail, particularly because of their teaching and learning methods and strategies:

We have quite a detailed literacy record because if you have reading with story books then you have to keep track of where children are and to inform teaching and learning.

Head teacher 5–7

Teaching children for whom English was a second language was a crucial issue for two schools:

80% of the children speak English as a second language. So it is important to record little bits of reading behaviour.

Nursery teacher

The record is also a good way to do justice to children's literacy development when English is their second language.

Nursery teacher

Keeping a child centred philosophy in teaching, learning and assessing was specifically highlighted by three schools:

We wanted to develop a system which kept children at the centre of assessment and kept process as well as subjects in view.

Head teacher 5–7

You have to see what children are learning, then assessment and record keeping is part of that.

Language co-ordinator 3–8

You need to build on what children can do – work from inside out not outside in.

Head teacher 3–7

The importance of ensuring that philosophy was 'in tune' with assessment was alluded to by several schools and mentioned specifically by one head teacher:

Records should match the philosophy. Many things – like tick boxes – don't do that.

Head teacher 3–7

Another head teacher felt that the assessment of literacy was a fundamental role of education:

I think literacy is fundamental, in our school we would be better thinking about good literacy assessments rather than being burdened with hundreds of Attainment Targets. You can tell from looking at a child's literacy how well they are doing generally.

Head teacher 3–11

Teachers' purposes for assessing and recording literacy

Teachers were asked what they felt to be the main purposes of assessing and recording children's literacy development. Eighteen different purposes for assessing and recording literacy were given and some teachers mentioned several purposes. These fall into two categories – Teaching and Policy – with six areas within those that were the main focus of comments (see Table 4).

The responses show that there are common concerns relating to teaching and other policy issues. These will be discussed later.

Literacy was regarded as important by most nursery teachers. Only three teachers said that for children under five literacy was not relevant. One said that she did not think about purposes of assessment in this area, the other specified what she felt it was inappropriate to assess. Such views reflect the traditional view of literacy held by nursery teachers and reflected in studies by Taylor *et al.* (1972) and Hannon and James (1990).

> It's a bit early to look at literacy in detail, but early skills like matching, one to one, sorting and recognising shapes can be acquired and recorded.
>
> Nursery teacher

> Not to pressure them into learning something that is better left until later. We do a lot of emergent literacy – good quality books and lots of writing in play. I have a worrying thought that we might be doing too much – if we do all this in nursery – what will happen in school? This downward pressure is on us all the time, so we do it in planning and play but it shouldn't be assessed in nursery, it's too much.
>
> Nursery teacher

> It's not literacy as such, but the early skills which children develop. We don't have a literacy record, they are too young for that, some of them can't hold a pencil when they begin nursery. So it's a bit early for a literacy record. It would be full of blanks. In nursery it isn't relevant really, so it's not something I would think about.
>
> Nursery teacher

These opinions are in accordance with the views of nursery teachers in a study of nursery education carried out in the early 1970s (Taylor *et al.* 1972), which found that nursery teachers saw the development of oral language skills as of high importance (p. 42) but whilst some nursery

Table 4　Teachers' purposes for assessing and recording early literacy

Teaching or policy	Purpose	Specific comments for children's and reasons	No. of responses
Policy	*Accountability*	• accounting for children's progress	5
		• external pressure of teacher performance and accountability	5
		• legal duty	1
Policy	*National Curriculum*	• levels of attainment (for 5+)	2
		• track child's development in relation to NC (5+)	6
Teaching	*Child's progress*	• keeping track of development	18
		• to check progress is OK	4
		• to get picture of what a child can do	5
		• to record child's skills	1
		• see which reading book they're on	1
Teaching	*Diagnostic*	• spot differences early	1
Teaching	*Parents*	• for parents to see child's development	2
		• for parents to contribute to learning and development	2
Teaching	*Teaching and learning processes*	• supporting teaching and learning	8
		• progression (including 'passing on' records)	10
		• continuity	6
		• a planning tool	4
		• to ensure curriculum match for each child	3

teachers saw the development of early mathematical concepts as part of their role (p. 88) there was no suggestion that they should play a similar role in terms of early literacy development.

The survey indicated that the majority of nursery teachers held different views of literacy to those expressed by a few of their colleagues. This group spoke of literacy in ways which were in tune with current research and with national policy of the early 1990s (DES, 1990a, 1990b).

> I'm interested in emergent literacy, we have a lot of children in the early stages of writing.
>
> Nursery teacher

> With young children it is part of everything, early drawing, talking – so literacy and language is a main focus in nursery education.
>
> Nursery head teacher

> It's really important to record children's literacy development in the early stages.
>
> Deputy head teacher 3–11

> I think early literacy development is becoming more and more important.
>
> Nursery teacher

> We're really into literacy here!
>
> Nursery head teacher

Emergent literacy and early development is so important – we need to do something about it here in the nursery

Deputy head 3–12

Teachers saw three main teaching and learning purposes for assessing literacy:

- to track, map or plot development
- as a diagnostic process which aided curriculum planning and teaching interventions
- for National Curriculum Assessment.

i. Tracking, mapping and plotting development

The notion of tracking development as it happened seemed popular with nursery teachers. This conveyed a child centred approach to assessment and record keeping, recording what happened when it happens, rather than using a checklist to plot predetermined targets or actively investigating to see if a child has certain knowledge, skills or understanding. Teachers said things like:

So that you know where each child is.

Nursery teacher

Keeping track of where the child is and relate to National Curriculum.

Head teacher 3–8

We keep a check and then can help them along.

Nursery teacher

On a single sheet we record skills: pre-reading, pre-maths, like sorting, matching, colours and so on.

Nursery teacher

To have a basis of where they are – their reading – with younger children you can see it in their work.

Infant co-ordinator 5–11

These comments convey the feeling of *following the child* with some interest, but do not in themselves suggest a further role for the teacher in extending children's present knowledge. However, this is reflected in the second aim – of assessment to aid teaching and learning.

ii. To aid teaching and learning

Some teachers felt that assessment and record keeping was important to the teaching and learning process and should be carried out in order to ensure that the curriculum was matched to children's developmental needs.

In nursery it is to build up a profile of their development and spot any difficulties early.

Nursery teacher

To plot development and to plan for the next bit of teaching and experiences the child needs to progress.

Nursery head teacher

Literacy is the only subject based record, developed because of a change in reading methods. So that the record is an aid to teaching and learning.

Head teacher 5–7

To monitor and support and extend children's literacy development.

Head teacher 3–7

Not all believed that assessment and record keeping would aid teaching and learning, but felt that they should reflect on and describe the development of a set of complex behaviours:

We have done a lot of work on early literacy, emergent writing and all that in curriculum, and we do a lot of talking with parents about literacy but we don't have a separate record. I don't feel at this age that we need it. I feel that records should be a summary really – and very brief.

Nursery head teacher

iii. National Curriculum Assessment

Teachers made a number of comments about reasons for assessing imposed by the National Curriculum. All schools with children aged five and over recorded attainment targets on some form of checklist.

In school it's all about targets now, and making sure everyone is at level 2!

Nursery teacher

National Curriculum attainment targets are too broad to inform teaching and learning.

Head teacher 5–7

I don't think the National Curriculum attainment targets are good enough. There is much more to becoming literate than that – it just shows what is valued, not what steps children need to take. Those attainment targets don't help teaching and learning, they're just a formality.

Nursery teacher

The attainment targets for English in the National Curriculum are not helpful in teaching and learning of children's literacy because they are far too broad.

Infant language co-ordinator

We have detailed records for literacy (and maths and science), because the National Curriculum Attainment targets checklists are not enough. We were thinking and working on literacy before the National Curriculum. It is development which is important, so we have fitted the National Curriculum in around how children learn.

Head teacher 3–8

One school had felt a serious effect of the National Curriculum Assessment:

We've changed our minds six times in the last three years. Whatever we do doesn't seem to work for us. We can't decide on a system which is workable, legal and realistic in terms of what to record and the time it takes to do it. All we can manage, having tried so many times, we've now gone for recording just National Curriculum requirements. Sad really, but what can we do? There is so much to record, we decided to do what is legally needed.

Head teacher 3–11

Some nursery teachers were clear to point out that they did not need to teach or to assess in terms of the National Curriculum.

We are not bound by the National Curriculum – it's about development in nursery – not targets.

Nursery head teacher

The National Curriculum does not apply to nursery children – we have not yet bowed to the pressures to assess in terms of National Curriculum.

Nursery teacher

Other nursery teachers felt that the National Curriculum had an effect on teaching and assessing in the nursery:

The National Curriculum has had an influence. I suppose really (on nursery literacy assessment). We've had to develop a record which is useful throughout the school. Attainment targets don't help especially where children speak English as a second language.

Nursery teacher

Bilingualism was again an assessment issue:

The National Curriculum does not really take account of the fact that children can be very able and literate in their home language, yet at a different stage in English.

Head teacher 3–7

The comments reveal a sense of concern that the National Curriculum for 5–16 year olds would eventually filter down and pressure in terms of a nursery curriculum designed to prepare children for the National Curriculum at five years was feared but resisted. These concerns were realised in September 1995 when the School Curriculum and Assessment Authority published draft proposals that became the basis for funding nursery education in January 1996 (DFEE/SCAA, 1996a). As discussed in Chapter 3, further confirmation of downward and political pressure came in September 1996 and again in early 1997, with the publication of government proposals for national baseline assessment at five years with literacy at the core (SCAA, 1996a; SCAA, 1997a). Such political moves clearly were to influence the shape of nursery education at the start of the twenty-first century, with emphasis on particular elements of literacy and numeracy. The implications of this move for early literacy assessment have already been discussed.

The impact of policy

Reaction to government policies

Many teachers' responses were influenced by the impact of recent government policies on assessment of seven year olds. Fifteen responses were directly concerned with government policy on assessment. These covered five main issues:

i   restriction of developments
ii. effects of school inspections
iii. parents' opinions
iv. overwhelming paper work and administration
v.   anger.

i. Restriction of developments

The Education Reform Act (1988) has restricted work with parents because policy documents needed to be drawn up and agreed throughout the school. That took time. Also we lost a nursery teacher under LMS so all our flexibility has gone.

Nursery teacher

ii. Effects of school inspections

HMI said that this record is too much – too detailed, so we are thinking again about what to do.

Nursery teacher

We think this [way of assessing] does what we want it to do – we're just a bit unsure about whether what we want it to do is 'right' in terms of government policy and HMI say.

Language co-ordinator 5–11

iii. Parents' opinions

The parents think that the testing was wrong – they felt that the children were too young (seven years and SATS).

Head teacher 3–8

So far as SATS are concerned we had a meeting for parents, they felt that the SATs were too time consuming and too much work for teachers to do – unnecessary work load. Parents felt pressure on teachers was unnecessary.

Head teacher 3–11

These views were reflected across the country. *Child Education* in August 1992 commented as follows on the second year of SATS for seven year olds in England and Wales:

> Few felt that the SATS had shown them much about children that they did not know already. It seems unlikely the community will learn much from SATS results about the real achievements of individual schools. Research among parents shows that the terminology has proved confusing, and contrary to political opinion, they are not all that keen to see publication of League Tables comparing schools.

(p.4)

iv. Overwhelming paperwork and administration

Teachers felt that paperwork was interrupting their teaching.

[We want] less paper coming at us.

Head teacher 3–7

I think it will settle down eventually. There are still so many changes going on. We're being asked to implement things whilst they are still being developed

Head teacher 3–7

A reduction in the pressure, a little is good but a lot is counter productive

Head teacher 3–11

Teachers have assessed children for years, but not according to agreed criteria, that is where we undersold ourselves, now we have this imposed and unworkable structure.

Head teacher 3–11

I would like to see the removal of restrictive impositions of assessment, like attainment targets which are meaningless. The removal of SATs would help

Head teacher 5–7

v. Anger at policies that create pressure

It is right to acknowledge the very real anger that many expressed. Such anger was due to several factors: the restriction of worthwhile experiences for children; pressure of newly imposed school inspections; lack of recognition of parents' stated opinions; and overwhelming paperwork which threatened the quality of classroom practice. Head teachers said:

An end to SATs and a return to proper teaching and learning. Assessment and record keeping is now so overrated, every other word is assessment.

Head teacher 3–8

We were always good record keepers and had good records of children's development in different areas. But since the National Curriculum, we've decided that we will record what the attainment targets – that is what they (the powers that be) are interested in. They seem to think that is what is important so that's what we're doing. We don't use our records now, since the National Curriculum.

Head teacher 3–8

Some of the assessment reforms are fine, but the government seems to be behaving like they invented assessment

Head teacher 3–12

We feel so angry that they way the National Curriculum was imposed, deskilled teachers, we're all going back to our skills now, now we've tried what was imposed to prove that it doesn't work.

Head teacher 5–7

Assessment as a means of accountability

A clear message from the survey was that schools and teachers saw newly imposed government requirements for assessment as a means of holding them accountable for the progress of children. There was not so much reluctance to be accountable, but a dismay at the criteria by which teachers felt they were being held accountable. There was also a feeling that National Curriculum Assessment was a way of appraising teachers' effectiveness:

In school now it [assessment and recording] is about levels, how many children have got to which point. It's not really now about children, it's more what teachers are doing.

Head teacher 3–7

In school there is more pressure, more towards accountability for teachers – teachers feel that unless children have got to level 2, they haven't done their job.

Head teacher 3–11

In school – now – it is about accounting for progress in terms of National Curriculum. It wasn't , and that wasn't how we felt about it – but now – with things being imposed – we account for children's progress through the National Curriculum.

Head teacher 3–11

The external purposes of assessment are really about the perfor- mance of teachers in the school – not the children. The attainment targets and SATs are the imposed assessments which are about accountability, not about teaching or children's learning – not really.

Infant language co-ordinator

For staff in school it is more about accountability now. They worry if children are not reaching level 2 before they do the SAT. Even though they have made really good progress in the two years.

Nursery teacher

On the one hand it is to account for what has been learned – to satisfy the law.

Head teacher 3–8

Most people keep records now because of the legislation and they need to know where the child is in relation to the National Curriculum.

Head teacher 3–8

The popularity of exploring the 'value-added' by a school to children's achievement gained currency during the 1990s and this trend has shown the teachers' views expressed above to be well founded. The teachers were right. National Curriculum Assessment led to league tables which were used to make judgements about school effectiveness. Assessment of early literacy as contained in proposals for Baseline Assessment (SCAA, 1996a, 1997a) was in danger of being driven by the desire for 'league tables' of results, rather than an appreciation of children's learning needs.

Teachers' assessment needs

Teachers identified three things that they needed to support their assess- ment work and to make it more effective:

- time
- in service education and training
- LEA support.

Time

From the sample of 30 schools, an overwhelming majority of 26 said that they would like more time to carry out appropriate assessments. They expanded upon their statement, giving twelve different reasons for needing more time to work on assessment.

They wanted more time :

1. to develop ideas
2. to reflect on children's work
3. for teachers to discuss children's assessments
4. for professional dialogue about assessment practice
5. and more help in the classroom
6. to think about children
7. to read about assessment and record keeping
8. to work on ideas about record keeping with parents
9. to observe children – meaningful observation
10. to liaise with the next school
11. for record keeping and assessment in general
12. to write comments on children's work.

The following comments indicate how teachers felt they would use any extra time:

> Just lots of time to really observe children and add details to records about what they can do – watching them write, or use a book, you can find out so much, so time to make really useful and meaningful observations.
>
> Nursery teacher

> Time . . . for professional dialogue . . . to talk with me as the head, somebody one step removed from the classroom – 'What do you mean by this?', 'What can I do about that ?', 'How can I check this?' – real professional dialogue.
>
> Head teacher 5–7

> Time . . . to really think about what children are doing, where we are going – what this piece of writing shows she has achieved, why I think that piece of writing is good.
>
> Head teacher 3–8

The need for time was therefore rooted in a professional desire to assess children effectively – observing, reflecting, discussing with colleagues, reading and considering next steps. Lack of time can limit the quality of assessments of children. One teacher was critical of her own practice:

> This record is not satisfactory to us – but it is what we can do under time constraints.
>
> Nursery teacher

In service education and training (INSET)

In addition to their comments about time, a number expressed the need for and usefulness of in service education and training on assessment and related issues. Their comments highlighted their need for more professional development opportunities around assessment and the effects that such experiences can have on the assessment of the young children they teach.

i. The need for INSET

Nursery teachers identified their own need for specific INSET in the literacy development of three to five year old children.

> I wish we had more courses for nursery teachers – they were so good.
>
> > Nursery teacher

> We need someone . . . to lead a day on assessment – to steer it along – a whole day to set us off.
>
> > Nursery teacher

> I just wish we could have some more courses on literacy development. We could do more on records of literacy too – more detail.
>
> > Nursery teacher

ii. The effect of INSET

Where there had been opportunities for INSET, there was some evidence of its usefulness in developing practice. Teachers commented on the impact of their own new learning on children's enhanced achievements:

> We've really got going with it – you can see the children filling in forms, writing little orders – it looks like writing too – it's just like . . . on that course.
>
> > Nursery teacher

> One of the nursery nurses devised a record after attending an in service post qualification course.
>
> > Nursery teacher

> Once on a course about assessment the course leader said to me – 'before you do it – think about what it is for – what it should do'. I often think about that – I think we know what our records are for and what they should do. I often think about what she said. At the time I wanted her to tell me what to do, but it was better really telling me to decide what I wanted.
>
> > Nursery teacher

The impact of higher degree courses is evident in the following comment. However, the withdrawal of funding and secondment opportunities for teachers to further their professional development has severely restricted this way of developing and influencing practice:

> I did all of this record in my own time as part of my M.Ed. study. Then we used staff meetings to discuss it.
>
> Nursery teacher

As the 1990s progressed much of the time available for professional development in the UK was taken up with courses that 'trained' teachers how to fill in particular forms and how to administer particular assessments and how to navigate their way through particular documentation to fulfil statutory requirements. In the latter half of the decade many LEAs attempted to provide a more balanced in service programme but teachers' opportunities to attend such courses were limited by school budgets and professional development had been eroded. National constraints and imposed initiatives had the effect of, as Hannon expressed it: 'bypassing teachers' thinking', (Hannon, 1997). Little room was left it seemed for teachers to *think* about their work as their time and energies were directed towards *implementing* externally devised plans.

LEA support

In addition to the need for INSET, the role of the LEA in providing support and implementing initiatives drew comment from fifteen teachers:

> We use the LEA record on literacy development . . . I'll look at the new LEA records too . . . I've got ideas now, with the new LEA under fives record.
>
> Nursery teacher

> We are about to start using the LEA record pack issued to schools. I shall find that very helpful in implementing a new recording system.
>
> Nursery teacher

> The new LEA record is so detailed – I've no time to do that.
>
> Nursery teacher

> The Literacy Group has been good for developing ideas on literacy.
>
> Nursery teacher

> The new LEA pack is unwieldy – there is too much blank space to write in.
>
> Nursery teacher

> We're really into literacy and it's all those courses and talking about it. We used parts of the LEA pack too. It's quite a new area in the

nursery, the idea of early reading and writing. I'm quite new to it all but enthusiasm of other people is infectious especially when people are always talking about it!

Nursery teacher

In my school I need LEA support, publications and discussion.

Nursery head teacher

Teachers evaluated the usefulness of LEA materials for themselves and were able to use these as springboards for specifically developed materials in their own schools.

Record keeping and assessment documentation

Another source of data gathered during the survey was samples of the schools' record keeping documentation. Twenty of the 30 schools offered copies of their current documentation. Of the 20 sets of documentation, 16 had record keeping documentation with a clear literacy focus, 18 favoured a checklist format, 10 used forms of observation and (not surprisingly) none used testing as a means of assessing children's early literacy development. Observation notes and observation according to checklists of developmental criteria were primary modes of early literacy assessment in the early 1990s.

The survey of teachers' purposes and practices in literacy assessment in one LEA indicates that there was amongst teachers in the early 1990s strong agreement on the need to assess early literacy development, and a deep professional concern that it should enhance their teaching and children's learning. It was also clear was that teachers have a range of assessment practice and procedures available to them. Their comments also indicated their perceived need for effective measures with which to challenge adverse and unrepresentative media and government reports on children's abilities in this field. Two nursery teachers' comments about the usefulness of research:

I think observing children is important for recording and assessing. Observations are also useful in terms of research – there is a place for more research into literacy in the nursery.

Nursery teacher

It's good to hear about research backing up what we believe.

Nursery teacher

What is clear is that teachers in the early 1990s did not use formal measures of literacy and one strong reason for this is likely to be – as Chapter 4 illustrated – that the suitability of existing measures is in doubt. The search for ways of measuring children's reading and writing abilities at seven years, as required in the National Curriculum, has resulted in numerous changes where no one is satisfied. Teachers felt dissatisfied with the tests, administration and criteria and politicians did not have the benchmarks they hoped the introduction of the National Curriculum and assessment arrangements would give them, but nevertheless used what they had. After huge public expenditure and hurried trials and development phases an imposed compromise resulted in 1992.

The survey of practice and purpose presented in this chapter showed that one overwhelming need of teachers was time. Given the emphasis on time needed for teachers to complete the proposed baseline assessment (SCAA, 1997a) there is every reason to suppose that teachers' concerns about time for assessment remain. It is clear that teachers and current practice are catered for in terms of assessment procedures and record keeping processes. However, teachers will always need adequate time to carry out assessment with proper respect for children and their learning: assessment which diagnoses learning needs and identifies areas for teaching plans.

7

A New Measure for Research in
Early Literacy Development

There is a richness of thinking about the purpose of assessment and the range of materials used by teachers confirms the argument that researchers, not teachers, are behind in the field as far as measurement of early literacy is concerned. If the problem was imagined in terms of a marathon race, teachers' knowledge and assessment practice would be three quarters of the way through the course whilst researchers would be still completing their entry form (or deciding whether to run or not!).

The urgent need is clear. Instruments to assess early literacy development must be devised that will enable researchers to measure children's emergent and developmental literacy in terms of environmental print, knowledge of books and early writing. Such instruments could enable researchers to measure literacy in ways more compatible to their research focus and more in step with current research in which present recognition of early literacy development is based.

This chapter provides a rationale for the development of a new measure for early literacy research – the Sheffield Early Literacy Development Profile. The design of the Profile and some aspects of its development are discussed and its characteristics are summarised. A report of a comparative appraisal of the Sheffield Early Literacy Development Profile and the LARR test of Emergent Literacy concludes the chapter.

Rationale

New views of early literacy development (Chapter 2), a review of three decades of measuring and assessing early literacy development (Chapter 4), a consideration of the purposes of such assessment (Chapter 5) and a survey of early literacy assessment practice (Chapter 6) point to the need for better assessment instruments for specific research purposes. In developing this new measure it was important to remember the perspectives discussed in earlier chapters. The most influential are briefly highlighted again.

Teale (1990) stated that

Formal tests impose the greatest restrictions on performance since their items tend to be specific and the range of acceptable answers, narrow.

(p. 46)

Teale suggests that selected performance sampling might strike a balance between formal testing and informal observation. He argues that tests do not measure 'all the right things' (p. 48), and that the 'focus on parts does not measure what emergent literacy emphasises' (p. 49). This reinforces the argument that what is measured should be determined by what we know about early literacy. Context is crucial and therefore any valid measure must set the context, purpose and audience.

The informal assessment advocated by Teale is probably the best type of balanced assessment and it can be carried out by teachers. Researchers can sometimes carry out such assessments during longitudinal studies, but also need a quick, reliable and valid measure against which their interventions can be viewed.

There are many factors to bear in mind when developing a measure of early literacy development that matches the findings of recent research. Sulzby (1990) discusses the following in relation to early writing: 'closeness' to conventional writing, context (writing is variable across contexts), wording, motivational aspects (is the child trying and does the teacher encourage or discourage?), open-ended nature of writing task, need for multiple assessments, one child, time of 'onset', scribble, drawing, nonphonetic letter strings, copying of conventional print, invented spelling, producing conventional print, rebus, aberration, pseudoletters, idiosyncratic forms. The list continues with Armstrong's concerns about assessing writing (1990), assessing the 'whole' rather than the constituent parts, narrative and illustration, patterns of intention, interests, motifs, orientations, interplay between form and content, technique and expression, relationship of word to picture, and meaning.

The above list can be supplemented if we consider aspects of assessing reading and environmental print. Heibert (1983) suggests that factors include: identifying an activity as reading, and identifying that print is necessary for reading. Goodall (1984) adds, ability to identify environmental print, context of print, letter knowledge. Goodman and Altwerger (1981) considered that important factors included: identification of logos, attitudes to reading and writing, knowledge of books, familiarity with books. Teale (1990) considered that a child's concept of the function of literacy was crucial.

Clearly the factors identified above generate a considerable list of issues to take account of when developing a tool to measure early literacy development. This list illustrates that effective measurement is complex. No assessment instrument can embrace the entire range of issues. However, in the development of new measures it is important to keep a sense of the complexity of issues that abound and attempt to embrace what is feasible within one instrument. It must be recognised that some ideas (such as those suggested by Armstrong) cannot, and perhaps should not, be included in a *measure* of literacy that attempts to quantify children's literacy behaviour and give it a score. To attempt to score 'meaning' would be an anathema, such attributes of children's writing deserve to be fully *appreciated* by knowledgeable teachers to the point where they are not assessed but are noted and nurtured.

The Sheffield Early Literacy Development Profile is a new measure of early literacy. It is called a 'Profile' rather than 'assessment', or 'test' because the term best describes the sampling of literacy behaviour that it will measure. The term 'Profile' also suggests a more 'rounded' approach rather than a narrowly focused view.

The Sheffield Early Literacy Development Profile has been developed with an appreciation of the complexity of the task. Its design and description is now presented and discussed.

Design of the Sheffield Early Literacy Development Profile

Purpose

The Sheffield Early Literacy Development Profile has been developed to indicate performance in aspects of early literacy development of children aged three to five years. Its design provides a means of comparing Profile scores of individuals and groups and over a period of time. The Profile complements rather than replaces other ways of finding out about children's early literacy development. It should *never* be viewed as a replacement for ongoing teacher assessment which, done well, is the best way of understanding children's literacy development.

For use by researchers

The Profile has been devised mainly for research purposes, though, as it engages children in real literacy tasks, and provides some detail of specific literacy behavious it may well reflect teachers' ongoing individual assessment processes. It samples performance in three strands of literacy – environmental print, books and writing – providing an indicator of children's performance on a sample of early literacy tasks. Sample behaviours relate to research in those same three areas. The Profile is not necessarily diagnostic because it *samples* literacy behaviour in key areas and is not sufficiently comprehensive to be used as a way of identifying the next step in teaching and learning. The Profile could have a role in indicating where further, more detailed observation and assessment might be needed, but existing strategies such as First Steps (Education Dept of Western Australia, 1994, 1994a) the Primary Language Record and the Barrs *et al.* (1989) Manchester Framework for Assessment (Manchester, 1989) are better tools for this purpose.

Features of the Profile

- The Profile can be administered on several occasions over a two year period with little likelihood of children becoming 'practised' in the tasks and achieving increased scores as a result.
- Scoring allows for a range of abilities from three year olds who are somewhat 'new' to literacy to children who are almost five with many literacy accomplishments.
- The Profile provides an indication of changes in performance if administered at intervals over two years.
- The Profile provides for useful comparison of a child's performance at different ages or stages, for example before and after an initiative. The Sheffield Early Literacy Development Profile could also be used in comparing cohorts of children, for example a group participating in a literacy project or programme with a comparison or control groups.
- The Profile covers three main areas of literacy: environmental print, book knowledge, writing.
- All three parts of the Profile are of equal importance – there is no weighting which suggests that some literacy behaviours are more important in early literacy than others and the three sub-tests can be used independently.
- All three parts of the Profile can be used, in which case the Profile would have three parts. Alternatively, researchers focusing on one strand of literacy, for example book knowledge, could use the appropriate part of the Profile alone.
- The Profile can be carried out by a researcher and scored on the Profile score sheet. In addition, teachers (or parents) might complete a separate assessment of the child's performance of the same areas, outside the 'test situation', such as the child's writing during play situations, or at home; their use of environmental print at the shops and so on. Scores in this case would be of less importance than the qualitative data the broader assessment provided.
- The Profile is not *necessarily* diagnostic. At this stage of early literacy all literacy behaviours of young children can be seen as positive behaviour and learning. There is no suggestion here that children who score low on the Profile have any difficulty or need extra help. The years three to five are a period of rapid development in literacy, the Profile would indicate which elements of literacy the child did or did not do at the time the Profile was administered. Though a low score may indicate

some areas where a child might benefit from more experiences, further observational assessments would be needed to diagnose learning needs and plan any useful teaching.

Administration

The Profile is administered on a one to one basis with the tester and child in whatever setting the child is comfortable. This can be at home, in a quiet room or a corner of a busy nursery, but it is important that there are no distractions. The Profile can be used in a nursery or class group setting or at home. All Profiles should be administered on a one to one basis. Scoring and administration does not allow for group testing. Children must have the individual attention of the tester as they work through the Profile with the adult presenting, and recording a child's response to, one item at a time. In addition to the literacy materials listed in the Profile, a low table and two chairs are needed.

Scoring

- Scoring is straightforward. The individual child's score sheet indicates potential scores and gives a box in which to write the child's score. Each of the three parts of the Profile carries a maximum score of 20 points.
- Maximum score 60 for the whole Profile; minimum score 0.
- High or maximum scores on each of the three parts of the Profile can be taken as an indicator of a balanced, all round development of key aspects of early literacy. Scoring can be completed on the score sheet. It provides a 'see at a glance' scoring system.

Time

There is no time limit but trials showed that the Profile and score sheets take an average of twelve minutes to complete. Unless the child refuses for whatever reason, the whole Profile is completed for each child regardless of the time they take.

Description

This section describes each task in the Sheffield Early Literacy Development Profile with reasons for inclusion. The final design of items in the Profile was based on appraisal of the materials by 15 teachers and an analysis of the performances of 100 children during three trial and development phases.

The Profile is in three parts:

Part One   Environmental Print

Part Two   Book Knowledge
Part Three   Early Writing.

Each part can be used independently or all three can be administered at once to provide a fuller 'Profile'.

Tasks in each part of the Profile, with their objectives, are now described in turn.

Part One: Environmental Print

There are three tasks in this part of the Profile:

Task 1 *Identifying Print in the outdoor environment* – is designed to find out if children can recognise from colour photographs of street scenes, forms of environmental print and say what they are for.

Task 2 *Identifying words and logos* – is designed to find out four things: whether children can recognise products from their packaging, whether they can identify words (from pictures) and whether they know any of the words in the text on the packaging and whether they can identify specific words in context. Five logos have been chosen to give children a fair chance of scoring some points on this section. A set of cards showing logos from five best selling products including: cereals, drinks, foods and household materials is used.

Task 3 *Decontextualised Print* – focuses on decontextualised environmental print and provides the opportunity to identify those children who are able to read words from familiar packaging without the clues and cues of context, design and colour. Reading 'Weetabix' from the Weetabix box is a different ability to reading the word 'Weetabix' printed in bold black letters on plain white card. Researchers have shown that children find this a more difficult task than 'reading' context based print (Jones and Hendrickson, 1970; Goodall, 1984). Some children are not at this point in their literacy development but the task has been included because a small number of children, particularly those at the upper end of the three to five age span or those with a wide experience of print, may be able to read some decontextualised print.

Part Two: Book Knowledge

Part Two of the Profile is concerned with book knowledge, a fundamental element of all children's early literacy development. It is surprising that, unlike those assessments developed by teachers, few researchers have actually used books to assess what children know about books. There are two tasks in this part.

Task 1 *Knowing about books* – focuses on children's ability to identify first the book itself and then certain features within it. Some items in this task draw on Clay's 'Concepts about Print' test (Clay, 1972a) but it also includes easier items because this Profile is designed for a younger age range than the target group for Clay's test. Unlike Clay's test, the Sheffield Early Literacy Development Profile uses childen's story books with a clear story line and words and pictures on each page. Criteria for selection of the books used and some examples are included in the Profile.

Task 2 *Using books – retelling stories* – is designed to provide an indication of children's ability to retell a story after looking through a book. This indicates children's ability to draw information from a book and to use pictures, and perhaps words, to retell the story in their own words.

Part Three: Early Writing

There are four tasks in the third and final part of the Profile which concerns early writing. Children's early writing behaviours have often begun by three years but there are no ways available to researchers for assessing knowledge about writing or writing itself for the youngest age range.

Task 1 *Identifying and knowing about writing* – focuses on the extent to which children know what writing is and what it is for.

Task 2 *Writing* – requires the child to do some writing of their own so that abilities such as: making a line of marks on paper, writing conventionally recognisable letters, and use of directionality can be assessed. They are asked to write something for a teddy bear (who is included to encourage the child to write), and finally they are asked to write their name. Trials showed that most children needed no encouragement to write but teachers found that the teddy bear was useful for those few children who, at this point, needed an added incentive to complete the task.

Task 3 *Writing words* – asks children to write some words they know. A similar item features in Clay's Diagnostic Survey designed for children over five years of age (1972). The items in the Sheffield Early Literacy Development Profile and the scoring for these items takes account of the young age range for which the Profile is designed, and whilst these abilities are recognised as part of writing development the earlier items (tasks 1 and 2 in part 3) are included to emphasise the earliest behaviours that are a fundamental part of beginning writing development.

Task 4 *Writing letters* – asks children to write all the letters they know. Letter and alphabetic knowledge is another part of early literacy developmen but the knowledge of letters as separate elements is difficult for very young children. Writing letters is included as the final task in the writing part of the Profile because some children will be able to demonstrate ability in letter writing.

There are a number of ways in which task 4 could be scored. If this Profile was intended for teachers the most useful information is how many letters children can write, which ones they know and use and which they have yet to learn. Some researchers looking for a final score may need different information, therefore a scale for scoring, sympathetic to the age and different developmental stages of children in the age range, has been developed. Figure 2 shows the numbers of letters written and the frerquency of each (n = 25, maximum possible score = 52).

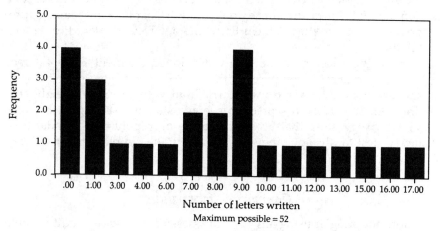

Number of letters written
Maximum possible = 52

Figure 2   Frequency of the number of letters written

Trials established that task 4 was difficult for many children and Figure 2 shows that on a sample of 25 children aged 3;1–4;11, the maximum number of letters written was 17. The scoring system below offers the potential for high scores but also gives recognition to children who are just beginning to include letters in their writing.

Letters written	points scores
1–5	1
6–10	2
11–15	3
16–25	4
26–32	5
32–45	6
46–52	7

Maximum score 7 points

The tasks of the Sheffield Early Literacy Development Profile summarised here are presented in detail with a copy of the score sheet in Appendix 1.

Comparative appraisal of the Sheffield Early Literacy Development Profile

There is only one published and standardised test which purports to measure emergent literacy – the LARR test of Emergent Literacy (NFER, 1993) which is intended for use with children aged from 4 to 5;3. The LARR test was gaining currency in the 1990s as a measure of early literacy and was in use during the later 1990s by researchers and teachers, had been adopted by some LEAs as a 'baseline' measure, and was used by the newly established National Literacy Project. Despite the reservations about the measure already discussed in Chapter 4, it seemed appropriate to compare the Sheffield Early Literacy Development Profile with LARR.

In order to test how the newly developed Sheffield Early Literacy development Profile compared with the LARR test of emergent literacy a small comparative exercise was carried out with a sample of eight children. All the children scored an average standardised score (between 93–115), suggesting that according to the only published standardised literacy test for the age range the children in the sample were of 'average literacy ability'.

Comparing 'face validity'

Before adopting or using any form of assessment the face validity should be appraised. Teachers, researchers and others look at the test and the items it includes and make some kind of judgement about its validity 'on the face of it'. The face validity of the Sheffield Early Literacy Development Profile has been discussed in detail earlier in this chapter and the theoretical base upon which it was constructed is clear.

The LARR test can be appraised according to the same theoretical position as that upon which the Sheffield Early Literacy Development Profile was constructed. The LARR test asks children to *identify*, by drawing a circle around, various pictures, letters, words or punctuation. It does not ask children to interpret environmental print, to use a book or to write (other than to draw a circle). The face validity of this test as a measure of emergent literacy is weak if it is appraised in terms of three key strands of emergent literacy that form the basis of this book. Figure 3 summarises the characteristics which earlier chapters of this book define as important elements for early literacy development research measures.

Despite the weaknesses of the LARR test in terms of face validity and its limited usefulness in terms of the analysis above, the test is becoming more widely used and as it is the only published test of 'emergent literacy' the results of eight children on the SELDP and the LARR were compared.

The children worked through the LARR and the Sheffield Early Literacy Profile on two consecutive days – LARR in groups of 4 and the

Instrument	Sets tasks in meaningful context	Covers knowledge of environmental print	Covers knowledge of books	Covers early writing	Can be repeated	Has a scoring system	Suitable for research involving comparisons
Early Literacy Development Profile	✓	✓	✓	✓	✓	✓	✓
LARR test of Emergent Literacy	–	•	•	–	✓	✓	?

✓ adequate coverage   • minimal coverage   – not a feature

Figure 3   Evaluation of the focus and characteristics of the SELDP and LARR

SELDP individually. Figure 4 shows the children's scores for the SELDP and LARR plotted onto a scattergram. It would be reasonable to expect that two measures that purported to measure the same thing would produce similar patterns of scoring. Children with low scores on one measure would be likely to achieve low scores on the other, children reaching high scores on one could be expected to do similarly on the second. However, Figure 4 suggests that there is no discernible relationship between the SELDP scores and those for LARR. The child in the sample with the highest LARR score achieved the lowest score on the SELDP.

This analysis can be taken further, by examining the results in a different way. Figure 5 shows the children's scores on both tests in relation to each other. If two tests, intended for use with children of the same age and developed to measure the same things, are used with the same sample of children it would be reasonable to expect to find similar score patterns. This was not the case with these two measures, so there appears

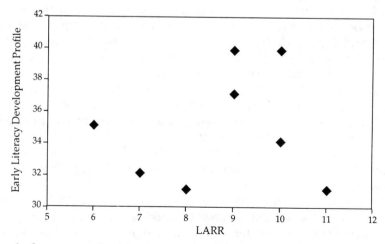

Figure 4   Scattergram showing scores for Sheffield Early Literacy Development Profile and LARR test of Emergent Literacy

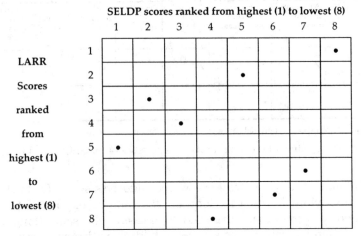

Figure 4   Comparison of rank scores on Sheffield Early Literacy
Development Profile scores with LARR raw scores (n = 8)

to be no relationship between LARR and the Early Literacy Development
Profile. If this is the case the LARR test and the Early Literacy
Development Profile are measuring different things. As the basis for the
latter is sound and it includes tasks which are based on observations of
children engaged in literacy in everyday contexts, and given the perceived
weaknesses in face validity of the LARR test it therefore questions
whether the LARR test is, as it claims to be, actually a measure of emergent literacy.

The information presented here was from a sample of eight, far too few
on which to base confident claims. The question about the extent to which
LARR measures what it purports to measure, and its comparison with
other measures of emergent literacy, remains a subject for future research.
However, this points to the need for careful appraisal of measures and an
approach to the selection of research instruments which is open to questioning what it is that measures of literacy *actually* measure.

The message from this comparative exercise is one of caution. Teachers,
researchers, policy makers and others interested in assessment and
measurement must approach the task of selecting tests and measures with
due care and attention. If tests do not measure what they say they measure
two questions are inescapable. What is the reliability of the measure?
What is the worth of the evaluations based upon the outcomes of such
measures?

Dangers lurk in the uncharted waters of early literacy testing, and there
is a danger that some instruments are used simply because they exist,
rather than because they offer what is needed. For example, the National
Literacy Project with its newly established Literacy Centres in Local
Authorities in the UK used LARR test in 1996 to assess literacy standards

of young children. Will the results of this apparently dubious test be used as evidence of the success or otherwise of the Literacy Centres' framework which included the 'literacy hour' initiative?

It is not sufficient for test distributors simply to assert that their product is 'a standardised test'. Standardised does not necessarily mean valid and it does not mean that the measure actually measures what it claims to measure. What matters is the basis upon which the test items have been developed which should be clearly discernible in the tasks children are asked to do.

The Sheffield Early Literacy Development Profile has not been standardised. Given the fluid nature of learning in the years before five, criterion referencing is an acceptable approach. The full text of the Profile booklet and Score sheet is in Appendix 1.

In the process of developing the Sheffield Early Literacy Development Profile, teachers involved in the trials reported that though the instrument was devised with a research focus in mind the format and content would yield interesting and useful information for them as teachers and that such an instrument could be useful to them as well as to those involved in research in the field. This is encouraging in that it suggests that the measure is in tune with best practice in teaching, and 'acceptable' in terms of what children are asked to do. However, it still remains that the best forms of assessment for teaching and learning involve teachers daily using a range of informal assessment strategies to build up a profile of their literacy including: observing children, reflecting on their work; talking with their parents; and talking with children. Teachers do not necessarily need quick measures.

End words

It is time to seek a more compatible relationship between assessment for teaching and learning and measurement for research.

Teachers have learned lessons from research which has led them to develop their teaching in ways which enhance children's literacy learning.

Researchers can now learn lessons from teachers about how measurement of children's literacy for research purposes might be improved.

There is no obvious justification for the mystification of assessment and testing and no plausible reason why measurement for research cannot be as meaningful as the best forms of assessment used in the processes of teaching and learning.

Appendix 1
The Sheffield Early Literacy Development Profile

About the Sheffield Early Literacy Development Profile

- The Sheffield Early Literacy Development Profile has been developed to measure three strands of children's literacy: environmental print, book knowledge and early writing.
- The Profile is designed to be administered to individual children aged between 3;0 and 4;11 years. The best location is a private room away from distractions.
- Administration time takes an average of twelve minutes but can vary and there is no time limit. Children must be allowed the time they need to complete the tasks.
- A small number of children may be reluctant to participate at all – others may decide that they do not wish to continue when they are part way through.
- At no point should children be put under pressure to work through the Profile. Testers are advised to write 'discontinued' on the child's score sheet at the point where they stop administering the Profile.
- If children have completed one or two parts of the Profile these could be scored, but the total score cannot be calculated.
- The Profile can be administered on more than one occasion with little risk of children becoming 'practised', so there is the option to invite children to try again later should they be happy to do so.
- Parents should be asked for their informed consent before the Profile is used with their children. Every opportunity should be given to parents to discuss the outcomes of their child's performance on the Profile in the context of their overall learning.

Copyright © 1997 Cathy Nutbrown

Part One: Environmental Print

Task 1: Identifying print in the outdoor environment

Materials needed

Colour photograph of street scene including several examples of environmental print.

Instructions

Show the child the colour photographs of the street scene.
Ask the following questions in this order:
1. *What can you see in the picture?*
2. *Can you point to some signs, some words in this picture?*
3. *What are signs for?*
4. *Do you know what any of these signs say?*

Scoring

1. no score – this is a 'warm up' question
2. score 1 point
3. score 1 points for simple answer: roads, shops, bags   **OR**
    score 2 points for more detailed answer showing greater understanding or knowledge *showing the way, showing what's in the shop, telling you . . .*
4. score 1 point for one correct response   **OR**
    score 2 points for two or more correct responses

Maximum score for task E1   **5 points**

Record scores during the administration on the score sheet in the appropriate boxes.

Record the final score in the total column in the box marked PART 1 Task 1.

Copyright © 1997 Cathy Nutbrown

TASK 2: *Identifying words and logos*

Materials needed

Set of five cards showing logos from best selling products including:

- cereals
- drinks
- foods
- household tasks.

These may be chosen according to the top ten best selling products. For this measure the following tasks were selected in this way:

- Weetabix
- Coca Cola
- Walkers crisps
- Persil washing powder
- Fairy liquid.

The photographs should be mounted on separate cards.

Instructions

Show the child one photograph at a time.
Ask the following questions for each photograph:
1. *What is this?*
2. *Show me the word(s) here ?*
3. *What do the words say?*
4. *Show me the word that says . . .*   Weetabix
                                          Coca Cola
                                          Walkers
                                          Persil
                                          Fairy

Scoring

For each photograph score as follows

Question 1	PS 1 Point	*Description of use or purpose is acceptable for example 'breakfast ' is acceptable for Weetabix.*
Question 2	PS 1 Point	*Pointing at any words on the picture is acceptable – but not pictures.*
Question 3	PS 1 Point	*Approximation of the words on the package is acceptable for example 'crisps' is acceptable for 'Walkers crisps'.*
Question 4	PS 1 Point	*The exact word listed must be pointed to.*

Copyright © 1997 Cathy Nutbrown

Total possible 'raw' score for task 2 is 20. Divide the maximum score by 2.
Maximum final score for task 2   **10 points**
Record scores during the Profile on the score sheet in the appropriate boxes.
Record the final score in the total column in the box marked PART 1 Task 2

Copyright © 1997 Cathy Nutbrown

TASK 3: Decontextualised print

Materials needed

Five cards printed in clear bold type with decontextualised words selected from the five products already used from the environmental print examples (task 2).

Instructions

Shuffle the five cards.
Show the child each card in turn and ask:
  What does this say?

Scoring

Score 1 point for each word read correctly. No approximations are acceptable.
Record scores during the Profile on the score sheet in the appropriate boxes.
Record the final score in the total column in the box marked PART 1 Task 3.

Copyright © 1997 Cathy Nutbrown

Part Two: Book Knowledge

Task 1: Knowing about books

Materials needed

Three objects of which one is a book selected according to the criteria below e.g. a teddy, the book, another object (cup, ball, jigsaw).

Criteria for book selection

a. Pictures and print should be clearly differentiated and should appear together on the majority of pages.
b. The book should be 'unfamiliar', possibly newly published or at least not available in the nursery/group book stock.
c. There should be a clear story line which is also discernible from the illustrations with, where appropriate, repeated illustrations of key characters.
d. Text should include appropriate punctuation and at least full stops and capital letters.

Some books which fit these criteria

Butterworth, N. and Inkpen, M. (1992) *Jasper's Beanstalk*, London, Hodder Children's Books.
Dale, P. (1990) *Wake Up Mr. B!*, London, Walker Books.
Mangan, A. (1996) *Little Teddy Left Behind*, Hayes, Magi Publications.
Murphy, J. (1986) *Five Minutes Peace*, London, Walker Books.

Instructions

Arrange the three objects, one of which is the book, on the table.
Ask the following:
1. *Pass me the book please?*
2. Take the book from the child (or from the table if the child does not succeed with question 1).
   Do you know what this is for? What do we do with a book?
3. *Show me the front of the book.*
4. *Show me a page in the book.*
5. *Show me a picture.*
6. *Show me the words.*
7. *Show me just one word.*
8. *Show me just one letter.*
9. *Show me the letter 'c'* (tester say the letter name not sound).
10. *What letter is this* (point to a 'b').

Copyright © 1997 Cathy Nutbrown

11. *Show me a full stop on this page* (open the book at a page where there is a full stop).
12. *Show me a capital letter on this page* (open the book at a page where there is a capital letter).

Scoring

1. score 1 point for picking the book
2. score 1 point for a suitable answer, e.g. 'for stories', 'to read', 'for bedtime', or other such reply which suggests that the child knows what a book is for
3. score 1 point if front is identified correctly
4. score 1 point if page is identified correctly
5. score 1 point if picture is identified correctly
6. score 1 point if words are identified correctly
7. score 1 point if a single word is identified correctly
8. score 1 point if a single letter is identified correctly
9. score 1 point if a letter 'c' is identified correctly
10. score 1 point if the child says 'b' (name or sound acceptable)
11. score 1 point for correctly pointing to full stop
12. score 1 point for correctly pointing to capital letter.

Maximum score for Task 1   **12 points**

Record scores during the Profile on the score sheet in the appropriate boxes.

Record the final score in the total column in the box marked PART 2 Task 1.

Copyright © 1997 Cathy Nutbrown

TASK 2: Using books – retelling stories

Materials

The same book chosen according to specified criteria.

Instructions

Give the book to the child and say: I just need to tidy up a bit, would you like to look at this book while I do that, then you can tell me about the story. Give the child time to look at the book then ask:
Will you tell me about that book?
1. *Who is in the story?*
2. *How does the story begin?*
3. *What happens in the story?*
4. *How does it end?*

Scoring

1. score 1 point for mention of single character either by name or by description (*a teddy, a dolly, patch, mummy, baby, etc.*)   **OR**
   score 2 points for mention of two or more characters
2. score 1 point for brief description of the start of the story (e.g. *there was a lady with a dog, there was a postman*)   **OR**
   score 2 points for a fuller description giving more specific detail
3. score 1 point for a brief description of events (*they went to the sea side, they had a party*)   **OR**
   score 2 points for a more detailed description of the plot with events in the correct order
4. score 1 point for brief description of the ending (*they came home and went to bed, they found the dog*)
   score 2 points for a fuller description of the ending.

Maximum score for Task 2   **8 points**
Record score in the appropriate boxes.
Record the final score in the total box marked PART 2 Task 2.

Copyright © 1997 Cathy Nutbrown

Appendix 1

Part Three: Early Writing

Task 1: Identifying and knowing about writing

Materials

Five postcard size pictures: animals, a toy, child's drawing, blank piece of coloured card, adult writing.
Blank writing paper – fine tipped black felt tip pen.

Instructions

Write a few lines in front of the child.
Ask the following:
1. _Do you know what I am doing?_
2. _Do you know what writing is for?_

Put this writing out of sight of the child and move on to the next task.

Lay the five pictures out on the table in front of the child:

*   toy (no. 1)
*   animals (no. 2)
*   child's drawing (no. 3)
*   adult's handwriting (no. 4)
*   blank coloured card (no. 5)

Tester take care not to 'eye' point or give other clues about the correct choice here.
Ask:
3. _Which one of these is writing?_

Scoring

1. score 1 point for correct description (for example _you're writing_)
2. score 1 point for suitable answer e.g. _letters, cards, stories etc._
3. score 1 point for identifying the adult's writing (no. 4)
Maximum score for Task 1   **3 points**
Record scores during Profile on the score sheet in the appropriate boxes.
Record the final score in the total box marked PART 3 Task 1.

Copyright © 1997 Cathy Nutbrown

TASK 2: Writing

Materials

Writing paper
Black felt tip pen
Teddy bear with glasses to fit

Instructions

Ask the child if s/he thinks teddies can write. Introduce the teddy who is wearing glasses. Say *This teddy can't write very well but he can read when he wears these magic glasses.*

The use of the teddy is to make the administration of the writing part of the Profile more user friendly and to give the child some encouragement to write if this is needed.

1. Give the paper and pen to the child. Ask the child to write a message on the paper for the teddy to read. Let the child write, encourage this effort. If the child says that s/he can't write say that the teddy can read all sorts of writing so long as he wears his magic glasses. Suggest that the child 'pretend' to write if he/she insists they cannot. If the child refuses at this point say *OK, let's try the last bit*, and go on to the next part of the Profile.

When the child has finished his/her 'independent' writing (or if they refused):

2. Ask:

Will you write your name at the bottom so that teddy knows it is from you?

If the child has already written their name either let them repeat it if they wish or identify for you which is their name in the first piece of writing.

Scoring

Score the child's writing as follows **whilst the child is writing**:

1. Making any line of marks   score 1 point
    making letter-like marks   score 1 point
    writing conventional letters   score 1 point
    writing left to right   score 1 point
    writing top to bottom   score 1 point
2. Name writing **after the child has left**:
    full name written correctly   score 1 point   **plus**
    beginning name with a capital letter   score 1 point

Maximum score for Task 2   **7 points**
Record scores on the score sheet in the appropriate boxes.

Copyright © 1997 Cathy Nutbrown

TASK 3: Writing words

Materials needed

Writing paper
Black felt tip pen

Instructions

Give the child a piece of blank paper. Ensure that no words are visible.
Say:
Write down some words you know.
Give the child a maximum of 1 minute – stop before this if the child stops
or says he/she has done all they can.

Scoring

After the child has left:
(Words must be spelled correctly to score)
Score 1 point for writing 1 word in addition to their name
(if this is written again)   **OR**
Score 2 points for writing 2–4 words   **OR**
Score 3 points for writing 5 or more words
Maximum score   **3 points**
Record the score in the box marked PART 3 Task 3.

Copyright © 1997 Cathy Nutbrown

TASK 4: *Writing letters*

Materials and instructions

Give the child a new sheet of paper and a black felt tip pen and say:
Write all the letters you know.
If the child is unsure say:
Do you know some letters in your name, or the alphabet? – have a go.

Scoring

After the child has left check off the letters on the score sheet for Part 3 Task 4.
Score according to the following scale:

Letters written	points scored
1–5	1
6–10	2
11–15	3
16–25	4
26–31	5
32–45	6
46–52	7
Maximum score	**7 points**.

Record the score in the appropriate box marked PART 3 Task 4.
Record the final score in the total box marked PART 3.

Profile concludes

Thank the child.
Complete the Profile score summary on the final page of the score sheet.
Attach writing samples to the score sheet.
Ensure all details on the score sheet are complete.
Add any tester's comments.

Copyright © 1997 Cathy Nutbrown

Appendix 1

Score sheet

Early Literacy Development Profile – Score sheet – 1997 Version

Child's first name	
Date of birth	
Date of Profile	
Age at testing	years months

Note: PS = Possible score   AS = Actual score achieved by the child

Part 1: Environmental Print

Task 1: Identifying print in the outdoor environment

Show the child the set of colour photographs of street scenes. Ask the following in this order:

No.	Question	PS	AS
1	What can you see in the pictures?	0	
2	Can you point to some signs, some words, in the pictures?	1	
3	What are signs for? (simple 1) more detailed (2)	1 or 2	
4	Do you know what any of these signs say? (simple 1 detailed 2)	1 or 2	
Total		5	

Copyright © 1997 Cathy Nutbrown

Task 2: Identifying words and logos

	What is this?		Show the words		What do words say?		Word that says . . .		Total
Picture	PS	AS	PS	AS	PS	AS	PS	AS	Total
Weetabix	1		1		1		1		
Coca Cola	1		1		1		1		
Walkers Crisps	1		1		1		1		
Persil Washing Powder	1		1		1		1		
Fairy Liquid	1		1		1		1		

Raw total ☐

Divide by 2 for actual score ☐

Add the total scores for each row. Total all the scores in the total boxes on the right hand side of the table. Insert the 'raw' score. Divide by 2 for the actual score for Task 2. Maximum score 10 points.

Task 3: Decontextualised print

Word	PS	AS
Weetabix	1	
Coca Cola	1	
Walkers	1	
Persil	1	
Fairy	1	
Total	5	

Part 1: Environmental Print – Possible score 20 Child's score ☐

Copyright © 1997 Cathy Nutbrown

Part 2: Book Knowledge

Task 1: Knowing about books

No.	Question	PS	AS
1	Pass me the book please?	1	
2	Do you know what this is for? What do we do with a book?	1	
3	Show me the front of the book.	1	
4	Show me a page in the book.	1	
5	Show me a picture.	1	
6	Show me the words.	1	
7	Show me just one word.	1	
8	Show me just one letter.	1	
9	Show me the letter 'c' (say letter name).	1	
10	What letter is this (point to 'b')?	1	
11	Show me a full stop on this page.	1	
12	Show me a capital letter on this page.	1	

Maximum score 12 points

score	

Task 2: Using books, retelling stories

No.	Question	PS	AS
1	Who is in the story? (one character 1–2+ score 2)	2	
2	How does the story begin? brief description score 1 more detailed score 2	2	
3	What happens in the story? brief description score 1 more detailed score 2	2	
4	How does the story end? brief description score 1 more detailed score 2	2	

Maximum score 8 points

score	

Part 2: Book Knowledge – Possible score 20   Child's score

Copyright © 1997 Cathy Nutbrown

Part 3: Early Writing

Task 1: Identifying and knowing about writing

No.	Question	PS	AS
1	Tester writes in front of the child. Do you know what I am doing?	1	
2	Do you know what writing is for?	1	
3	Show the 5 cards: (1,2,3,4,5). Which one of these is writing	1	
Maximum score 3 points		score	

Task 2: Writing

Child does a sample of writing, score after the child has left the room as follows:

	PS	AS
Making any line of marks	1	
Making letter-like marks	1	
Writing conventional letters	1	
Writing left ro right	1	
Writing from top to bottom	1	
	score	

Ask the child to write his or her name, score as follows:

	PS	AS
Name correctly written	1	
PLUS beginning name with capital letter	1	
Maximum score 7 points	score	

Task 3: Writing words

		PS	AS
1 word written (spelled) correctly apart from own name	**OR**	1	
2–4 words written (spelled) correctly	**OR**	2	
5 words written (spelled correctly)		3	
Maximum score 3 points		score	

Copyright © 1997 Cathy Nutbrown

Appendix 1

Score sheet - Part 3 Task 4 *Write all the letters you know*

a   b   c   d   e   f   g   h   i   j

k   l   m   n   o   p   q   r   s   t

u   v   w   x   y   z

A   B   C   D   E   F   G   H   I   J

K   L   M   N   O   P   Q   R   S   T

U   V   W   X   Y   Z

Total number of letters written   ☐

Score (see scale below)   ☐

Name_____

Date _____

Scoring scale

Letters written	score
1–5	1 point
6–10	2 points
11–15	3 points
16–25	4 points
26–32	5 points
33–44	6 points
45–52	7 points

Copyright © 1997 Cathy Nutbrown

Task 3: Writing letters

Number of letters written		PS	AS
1–5	**OR**	1	
6–10	**OR**	2	
11–15	**OR**	3	
16–25	**OR**	4	
26–32	**OR**	5	
33–44	**OR**	6	
45–52	**OR**	7	
Maximum score	**OR**	7	

Part 3: Early Writing – Possible score 20   **Child's score**

Copyright © 1997 Cathy Nutbrown

Sheffield Early Literacy Development
Profile score sheet summary

Part	Focus	PS	AS
1	**Environmental Print**	**20**	
Task 1	Identifying print in the outdoor environment	5	
Task 2	Identifying words and logos	10	
Task 3	Decontextualised print	5	
2	**Book Knowledge**	**20**	
Task 1	Knowing about books	12	
Task 2	Using books – retelling stories	8	
3	**Early Writing**	**20**	
Task 1	Identifying and knowing about writing	3	
Task 2	Writing	7	
Task 3	Writing words	3	
Task 4	Writing letters	7	
Total score for Profile		**60**	

REMEMBER TO ATTACH THE WRITING SAMPLE TO THE SCORE SHEET

Tester's Comments
Note briefly any points which were of particular mention in the administration on this occasion e.g. anything you did which may have influenced the outcomes, any interruptions, the child refusing to continue and subsequent abandonment of the Profile etc.

Time taken to administer the Profile .... minutes,

This includes completing the score sheet when the child has left.

Administerd by .... Project ....

Copyright © 1997 Cathy Nutbrown

References

Armstrong, M. (1990) Another way of looking. *FORUM for the discussion of new trends in education* Vol. 33, no. 1, pp. 12–16.

Baghban, M. (1984) *Our Daughter Learns to Read and Write: A Case Study from Birth to Three.* International Reading Association, Newark, Delaware.

Barrs, M., (1990) The Primary Language Record: reflection of issues in Evaluation *Language Arts* Vol. 67, no. 3, pp. 244–253.

Barrs, M., Ellis, S., Hester, H. and Thomas, A. (1989) *The Primary Language Record.* Inner London Education Authority/Centre for Language in Primary Education, London.

Barrs, M., and Thomas, A., (1991) *The Reading Book.* Centre for Language in Primary Education, London.

Barton, D. (1994) *Literacy.* Routledge, London.

Bartholomew, L. and Bruce, T. (1993) *Getting to Know You: A Guide to Record-keeping in Early Childhood Education and Care.* Hodder and Stoughton, London.

Birchenough, C. (1914) *History of Elementary Education in England and Wales.* University Tutorial Press, London.

Bissex, G.L. (1980) *GNYS AT WRK : A Child Learns to Write and Read.* Harvard University Press, Cambridge, M.A.

Blatchford, P., and Cline, T. (1992) Baseline assessment for school entrants, *Research Papers in Education Policy and Practice* Vol. 7, no. 3, pp. 247–269.

Bradley, L. and Bryant, P. (1983) Categorising sounds and learning to read: a causal connection. *Nature,* no. 301, pp. 419–21

Bradley, L. and Bryant, P. (1985) *Rhyme and Reason in Reading and Spelling.* IARLD Monographs, no. 1, Ann Arbour, University of Michigan Press.

Brimer, A., and Raban, B. (1979) *Administrative Manual for the Infant Reading Tests.* Education Evaluation Enterprises.

Brooks, G., Foxman, D., and Gorman, T. (1995) Standards in literacy and numeracy: 1948–1994 *NCE Briefing, No. 7.* National Commission on Education, London.

Bruner, J. (1990) *Acts of Meaning.* Harvard University Press, London.

Burgess-Macey, C. (1994) *Assessing Young Children's Learning* in Keel P. (ed) (1994) Assessment in the multi-ethnic primary classroom. Trenth, Stoke-on-Trent.

Butler, D. (1979) *Cushla and Her Books.* Hodder and Stoughton, London.

Cato, V. and Whetton, C. (1991) *An enquiry into local education authority evidence on standards of reading of seven-year-old children.* A report by the National Foundation for Educational Research, Department of Education and Science, London.

Child Education (1992) Assess the Scottish Way? *Editors Comment – Child Education* Vol. 69, no. 8. pp. 4 & 7.

Chittenden, E. and Courtney, R. (1989) Assessment of young children's reading: documentation as an alternative to testing. In *Emerging literacy: young children learn to read and write.* Strickland, D.S. and Morrow, L.M., (eds) Delaware: International Reading Association.

Clay. M. (1972a) *The Early Detection of Reading Difficulties: a Diagnostic Survey.* Heinemann Education Books, Auckland, NZ.

Clay, M. (1972b) *Sand.* Heinemann Education Books, Auckland, NZ.

Clay, M. (1975) *What Did I Write?* Heinemann Education Books, Auckland, NZ.

Clay, M. (1979a) *Stones.* Heinemann Education Books, Auckland, NZ.

Clay. M. (1979b) *The Early Detection of Reading Difficulties: a Diagnostic Survey (2nd edn.)* Heinemann Education Books, Auckland, NZ.

Clay, M. (1993) *An Observation Survey of Early Literacy Achievement.* Heinemann Education Books, Auckland, NZ.

Clymer, T. and Barrett, T.C. (1983) *Clymer-Barrett Readiness Test* (CBRT). Chapman, Brook and Kent, USA.

Department of Education and Science (1978) *Primary Education in England: A Survey by HM Inspectors of Schools.* HMSO, London.

Department of Education and Science (1988) *English for Ages 5–11 – Proposals of the Secretary of State for Education and Science and the Secretary of State for Wales.* National Curriculum Council, London.

Department of Education and Science (1989a) *The Education of Children Under Five.* HMSO, London.

Department of Education and Science (1989b) *English in the National Curriculum.* HMSO, London.

Department of Education and Science (1990a) *Starting with Quality. The Report of the Committee of Inquiry into the Quality of Educational Experiences offered to Three- and Four-year Old Children.* HMSO, London.

Department of Education and Science (1990b) *The Teaching and Learning of Language and Literacy.* HMSO, London.

Department for Education (1995) *English in the National Curriculum.* HMSO, London.

Department for Education and Employment/School Curriculum Assessment Authority (1996a) *Desirable Outcomes for Children's Learning on Entering Compulsory Education.* Department for Education and Employment/School Curriculum and Assessment Authority, London.

Department for Education and Employment (1996b) *Nursery Education Scheme: The Next Steps.* Department for Education and Employment, London.

Desforges, M. and Lindsay, G. (1995) *The Infant Index.* Hodder and Stoughton, London.

Dickens, C. (1860) *Great Expectations.*

Downing, J., Ayres, D.M., and Schaeffer, B. (1983) *Linguistic Awareness in Reading Readiness (LARR).* National Foundation for Educational Research-Nelson, London.

Downing, J. and Thackray, D. (1976) *Reading Readiness Inventory.* Hodder and Stoughton, London.

Drummond, M.J. (1993) *Assessing Children's Learning.* David Fulton, London.

Durkin, D. (1966) *Children Who Read Early.* Teachers College Press, New York.

Dyson, A.H. (1984) Learning to write/learning to do school: Emergent writer's interpretations of school literacy tasks. *Research in the Teaching of English* Vol. 18, pp. 233–264.

Education Department of Western Australia (1994) *Writing Developmental Continuum.* Longman, Melbourne, Australia.

Education Department of Western Australia (1994) *Reading Developmental Continuum.* Longman, Melbourne, Australia.

Ferrerio, E., and Teberosky, A. (1982) *Literacy Before Schooling*. Heinemann, London.

Frederickson, N., Frith, U. and Reason, R. (1997) *Phonological Assessment Battery*. NFER-Nelson, Windsor.

Gardner, K. (1986) *Reading in Today's Schools*. Oliver and Boyd, Edinburgh.

Goodall, M. (1984) Can four year olds 'read' words in the environment? *Reading Teacher* Vol. 37, no. 6, 478–482.

Goodman, K. (1986) *What's Whole in Whole Language?* Scholastic, London.

Goodman, Y. (1980) The roots of literacy. *Claremont Reading Conference Yearbook*, 44, 1–12.

Goodman, Y. (1981) Test review: concepts about print tests. *Reading Teacher*, 34, 445–448.

Goodman, Y. and Altwerger, B. (1981) Print awareness in preschool children: a working paper. *A research paper*. September 1981 no. 4, University of Arizona.

Goodman, Y. and Burke, C. (1972) *The Reading Miscue Inventory*. New York, Macmillan.

Gorman, T and Fernandes, C. (1992) *Reading in Recession*. National Foundation for Educational Research, Slough.

Goswami, U, and Bryant, P. (1990) *Phonological Skills and Learning to Read*. Lawrence Earlbaum Associates, Hove.

Gravelle, M. and Struman, E. (1994) Assessment of bilingual pupils: issues of fluency. In Keel P. (ed.) (1994) *Assessment in the Multi-Ethnic Primary Classroom*. Trentham, Stoke-on-Trent.

Gregory, E. (1996) *Making Sense of a New World: Learning to Read in a Second Language*. Paul Chapman, London.

Hall, N. (1987) *The Emergence of Literacy*. Hodder and Stoughton, Kent.

Hall, N. (ed.) (1989) *Writing with Reason*. Hodder and Stoughton, London.

Hall, N. and Abbott, L. (eds) (1991) *Play in the Primary Curriculum*. Hodder and Stoughton, London.

Hall, N. (1991) Play and the emergence of literacy, in Christie, J. (1991) *Play and Early Literacy Development*.

Hannon, P. (1995) *Literacy, Home and School: Research and Practice in Teaching Literacy with Parents*. The Falmer Press, London.

Hannon, P. (1997) The future lies in the past, *TES* 24.1.97, pp. 13 and 16.

Hannon, P. and James, S. (1990) Parents' and teachers' perspectives on preschool literacy development. *British Educational Research Journal* Vol. 16, no. 3.

Hannon, P. and McNally, J. (1986) Children's understanding and cultural factors in reading test performance. *Educational Review*, Vol. 38, no. 3.

Harste, J.C., Woodward, V.A., and Burke, C.L. (1984) *Language Stories and Literacy Lessons*. Heinemann, Portsmouth, N.H.

Hartley, D.N. and Quine, P.G. (1982) A critical appraisal of Marie Clay's 'Concepts about Print' test. *Reading*, Vol. 6, no. 2, pp. 109–112.

Heibert, E.H. (1983) Knowing about reading before reading: preschool children's concepts of reading. *Reading Psychology*, Vol. 4, no. 3–4, pp. 253–260.

Hirst, K. (1997) Bilingualism and early literacy development. In Nutbrown, C. and Hannon, P. (1997) *Preparing for Early Literacy Education with Parents: A Professional Development Manual*. NES Arnold/REAL Project, Nottingham.

Hodgson, P. (1987) Writing and role play. *About Writing*, no. 5, p. 11.

Holdaway, D. (1979) *The Foundations of Literacy*. Ashton Scholastic, Auckland.

Huss, R.L. (1991) Among diverse worlds: an ethnographic study of young children becoming literate in a British multiethnic primary school classroom. Unpublished PhD dissertation, Georgia State University.

Jones, M., and Hendrickson, N. (1970) Recognition by preschool children of advertised products and book covers *Journal of Home Economics*, Vol. 62, no. 4, 263–267.

Keel, P. (ed.) (1994) *Assessment in the multi-ethnic primary classroom*. Stoke-on-Trent, Trentham.

Kent LEA (1992) *Reading Assessment Profile*. Kent County Council, Kent.

Lazo, M.G. and Pumfrey, P.D. (1996) Early predictors of later attainment in reading and spelling. *Reading*, Vol. 30, no. 3, pp. 5–11.

Lorenz, S., (1997) Foresight in funding in *TES, Extra Special Needs*, April 18 1997, p. III.

Manchester LEA (1988) *Early Literacy Project: A Framework for Assessment*. Manchester City Council Education Department

MacLean, M., Bryant, P. and Bradley, L. (1987) Rhymes, nursery rhymes, and reading in early childhood. *Merrill-Palmer Quarterly*, 33(3), pp. 225–281.

McGee, L., Lomax, R. and Head, M. (1984) *Young Children's Functional Reading*. Paper presented at The National Reading Conference, Florida.

Meek, M. (1988) *How Texts Teach What Readers Learn*. Thimble Press, Stroud.

Meek, M. (1991) *On Being Literate*. The Bodley Head, London.

Millard, E. (1997) *Differently Literate*. Falmer, London.

Mills, J. (1995) Bilingual children and their assessment through mother tongue. In *Working with Bilingual Children* Verma, M.K., Corrigan, K.P. and Firth, S. (eds) (1995). Multilingual Matters, Clevedon.

Mitchell, R. (1992) *Testing for Learning: How New Approaches to Evaluation Can Improve American Schools*. The Free Press, New York.

Morrow, L.M., and Smith, J.K. (eds) (1990) *Assessment for Instruction in Early Literacy*. Prentice Hall, New Jersey.

National Writing Project (1989) *Becoming a Writer*. Nelson, London.

Neuman, S. (1996) Is access enough? Examining the effects of a social-constructivist approach to family literacy on children's concepts and responses to literature. Paper presented at the American Educational Research Association, April 1996 New York, USA.

NFER-Nelson (1993) *LARR Test of Emergent Literacy: Teacher's Guide*. NFER, Windsor.

NFER-Nelson (1996a) *Trials of Baseline Assessment Schemes*, Report 1. NFER, Windsor.

NFER-Nelson (1996b) *Trials of Baseline Assessment Schemes*, Report 1. NFER, Windsor.

Nutbrown, C. (1996) *Respectful Educators – Capable Learners: Children's Rights and Early Education*. Paul Chapman, London.

Nutbrown, C. (1997) The place of early literacy education and parental involvement in national preschool curriculum policy and practice. In Nutbrown, C. and Hannon P. (eds) *Preparing for Early Literacy Education with Parents: A Professional Development Manual*. NES Arnold/The REAL Project, Nottingham.

Nutbrown, C. and Hannon, P. (1997) *Preparing for Early Literacy Education with Parents: A Professional Development Manual*. NES Arnold/REAL Project, Nottingham.

Nutbrown, C., Hannon, P. and Collier, S. (1996) *Early Literacy Education with Parents – A Framework for Practice*. REAL Project SUTV (Video) Sheffield, University of Sheffield, SUTV, 5 Flavell Road, Sheffield S3 7QX.

Payton, S. (1984) Developing awareness of print: a young child's first steps towards literacy. *Educational Review* Occasional Publications, no. 2. University of Birmingham, Birmingham.

Riley, J. (1996) *The Teaching of Reading*. Paul Chapman Publishing, London.

Robson, A., (1995) The assessment of bilingual children. In *Working with Bilingual Children* Verma, M.K., Corrigan, K.P. and Firth, S. (eds) (1995). Multilingual Matters, Clevedon.

Root, B. (1986) In defence of reading schemes. In Root, B. (ed.) *Resources for Reading –*

Does Quality Count? United Kingdom Reading Association/Macmillan, London.

Schickedanz, J.A. (1990) *Adam's Righting Revolutions.* Heinemann, Portsmouth, N.H.

School Curriculum and Assessment Authority (1993) *The National Curriculum and its Assessment – Final Report.* SCAA, London.

School Curriculum and Assessment Authority (1996a) *Baseline Assessment – Draft Proposals.* SCAA, London.

School Curriculum and Assessment Authority (1997a) *SCAA Consultation on Baseline Assessment.* SCAA, London.

School Curriculum and Assessment Authority (1997b) *SCAA Consultation on Draft Criteria and Procedures for Accreditation of Baseline Assessment Schemes.* Middlesex: March 1997. SCAA, London.

Sheffield Early Years Literacy Association (1991) *Telling, Reading and Writing Stories.* SEYLA, Sheffield.

Sheffield LEA (1996) *Baseline Assessment at School Entry – A Report on the Full Pilot of Baseline Assessment in Sheffield LEA Schools 1995–96.* Sheffield Education Service.

Simon, B. (1960) *Studies in the History of Education 1780–1870.* Lawrence and Wishart, London.

Siraj-Blatchford, I. (1996) Language culture and difference: challenging inequality and promoting respect. In Nutbrown, C. (1996) *Respectful Educators – Capable Learners: Children's Rights and Early Education.* Paul Chapman, London.

Smith, F. (1988) *Joining the Literacy Club.* Heinemann, London.

Strand, S. (1996) Value added analysis of the 1995 Key Stage 1 results: an LEA case study. Paper presented to the British Educational Research Association September 1996 Lancaster University.

Sulzby, Y, E., (1985a) Kindergarteners as writers and readers, in Farr, M. (ed) *Children's Early Writing Development.* Norwood, N.J.: Ablex Publishing Corporation.

Sulzby, E., (1985b) *Forms of Writing and Re-reading: Example List.* Unpublished examiners manual. Northwestern University, Evanston, IL.

Sulzby, E. (1990) Assessment of emergent writing and children's language while writing. In Morrow, L.M. and Smith, J.K. (eds) *Assessment for Instruction in Early Literacy.* Prentice Hall, New Jersey.

Sulzby, E. and Teale, W.H. (1985) Writing development in early childhood. *Educational Horizons*, Vol. 64, pp. 8–12.

Sylva, K. and Hurry, J. (1995) *Early Intervention in Children with Reading Difficulties : An Evaluation of Reading Recovery and a Phonological Training.* London: School Curriculum and Assessment Authority.

Taylor, P.H., Exon, G. and Holley, B. (1972) *A Study of Nursery Education.* Schools Council Working Paper 41. Evans-Methuen, London.

Teale, W.H. and Sulzby, E. (eds) (1986) *Emergent Literacy: Writing and Reading.* Ablex, Norwood, NJ.

Teale, W.H. (1990) The promise and challenge of informal assessment in early literacy. In Morrow, L.M. and Smith J.K. (eds) (1990) *Assessment for Instruction in Early Literacy.* Prentice Hall, New Jersey.

Temple, C., Nathan, R., Burris, N., and Temple, F. (1982) *The Beginnings of Writing.* Allyn and Bacon, Massachusetts.

Thackray, D.V. and Thackray, L.E. (1974) *Thackray Reading Readiness Profiles.* Hodder and Stoughton, London.

Tough, J. (1976) *Listening to Children Talking.* Ward Lock Educational, London.

Turner, M. (1990) *Sponsored Reading Failure.* IEA Education Unit, Warlingham Park School, Warlingham, Surrey.

Vincent, D., Green, L., Francis, J. and Powney, J. (1983) *A Review of Reading Tests.* National Foundation for Educational Research, London.

Vincent, D., Crumpler, M. and de la Mare, M. (1996) *Manual for Stage 1 of the Reading Progress Tests*. Hodder and Stoughton, London.

Walker, C. (1975) *Teaching Prereading Skills*. Ward Lock Educational, London.

Wandsworth Borough Council Education Department (1994) *Baseline Assessment Handbook*. Wandsworth LEA, London.

Wandsworth Education Department Research and Evaluation Unit (1995) *Wandsworth Baseline Assessment 1994/5*. Wandsworth LEA, London.

Waterland, L. (1985) *Read with Me*. Thimble Press, Stroud.

Waterland, L. (1989) *Apprenticeship in Action*. Thimble Press, Stroud.

Waterland, L. (1992) Ranging freely. In *After Alice – Exploring Children's Literature*. Styles, M., Bearne, E. and Watson, V. (1992). Cassell, London.

Wells, G. (1987) *The Meaning Makers: Children Learning Language and Using Language to Learn*. Hodder and Stoughton, London.

Whitehead, M. (1997) *Language and Literacy in the Early Years*, 2nd edn. Paul Chapman Publishing, London.

Woodhead, C. (1997) Do we have the schools we deserve? Annual Lecture by Chris Woodhead, Her Majesty's Chief Inspector of Schools in England, Tuesday 25 February 1997.

Wray, D., Bloom, W. and Hall, N. (1989) *Literacy in Action – the Development of Literacy in the Primary Years*. Falmer Press, London.

Ylisto, I (1977) Early reading responses of young Finnish children. *Reading Teacher*, November pp. 167–172.

Subject Index

Author Index

More Education Books from Paul Chapman Publishing

LANGUAGE AND LITERACY IN THE EARLY YEARS
Second Edition
Marian R Whitehead

This book has been revised and updated to reflect changes since it was first published – not only insights into language, literacy and child development, but also in huge new changes in the early years environment, such as the National Curriculum, desirable learning outcomes, baseline assessment and the just-4s in primary classrooms.

This new edition is relevant to a wide range of practitioners in early years settings. The author deals with a broad range of issues in language, literacy and learning, concentrating on the years 3–8 and on the professional interests of practitioners with this age-range. The author continues to reject quick-fix approaches to language and narrow prescriptive rules for teaching children, and re-asserts the complexity and the joy involved in supporting young children's development as speakers, writers and readers. Each chapter concludes with suggested further reading, and suggestions for teaching and learning.

This book is for teachers and practitioners in early years settings and primary schools, and for students training to work with the 3–8 age-group.

1 85396 341 0   *Paperback*   224pp   1997

DEVELOPING LANGUAGE AND LITERACY 3–8
Ann Browne, University of East Anglia

This book covers all aspects of a language and literacy curriculum for 3-8 year old pupils, including all four models of language, working with bilingual children, assessment, planning and policy-making. It is a practical and comprehensive guide to teaching and learning in the early years and includes examples from the classroom to illustrate particular approaches and organizational issues. Each chapter includes suggestions for further reading.

In writing this book the author has drawn from her extensive experience of working with student teachers, newly qualified teachers and teachers on in-service courses as well as her own experience as a teacher of early years pupils. This book will be of use to all these groups, and to any professional interested in the development of language and literacy in the early years of schooling.

User's Comments

'I like the layout and style of this book very much. It is straightforward and ideally suited to the needs of pre-service students.'

1 85396 282 1   *Paperback*   288pp   1996

MAKING SENSE OF A NEW WORLD
Learning to Read in a Second Language
Eve Gregory, Goldsmiths' College, University of London

How do young children go about learning to read in a new language? Is learning to read the same for monolinguals and emergent bilinguals? Or might the effort of simultaneously learning spoken and written English present special challenges for both child and teacher? These are some of the questions addressed in this book.

The author argues that talk, experience and reading in a second language are inextricably intertwined. She proposes an interactive model of reading within which emergent bilinguals have particular strengths and weaknesses as they call upon different 'clues' or cues. A knowledge of the strategies used by these children is essential in 'scaffolding' their learning.

The book includes practical approaches to teaching reading in the multilingual classroom, home/school reading programmes and recording children's reading progress. Throughout, discussions with children and their families, and observations and taped interactions in classrooms provide insights into the variety of reading practices in which emergent bilinguals already take part as they enter the new world of school.

The book includes a glossary, list of books to use and lesson-plans. It will be essential reading for early years and primary teachers of bilingual children.

'This book is not just for educators of emergent bilinguals, it is for all people interested in the teaching of language and reading to young children and because it provides food for thought on more than one occasion it is a book to be seriously considered.'
LANGUAGE AND LEARNING

'Making Sense of a New World deserves a place on the bookshelf of every primary teacher whose pupils are learning to read English as an additional language. It may not solve all the problems, but it will do more to help us understand them than any other book for teachers currently available.'
TES

1 85396 263 5   *Paperback*   208pp   1996

LITERACY GOES TO SCHOOL
The Parents' Role in Young Children's Literacy Learning
Jo Weinberger, University of Sheffield

Few primary teachers have a chance to find out in detail what children have already learnt, and continue to learn, about literacy at home. This book gives a clear demonstration of literacy learning at home, and how it differs from, as well as relates to, literacy at school. It will help teachers to increase their understanding of this process and to build on their relationship with parents. Such understanding, the book shows, can directly enhance children's literacy performance in school.

The book is based on the author's study of how more than 40 parents from a variety of backgrounds contributed to their children's literacy development. The author suggests practical ways for teachers to assess and develop their own practice. The book includes the author's Home-School Literacy Evaluation matrix, to help teachers review their contact with parents, and to promote and monitor change.

1 85396 292 9   *Paperback*   176pp   1996

RESPECTFUL EDUCATORS – CAPABLE LEARNERS
Children's Rights and Early Education
edited by Cathy Nutbrown

This book focuses on current early childhood issues and examines them in the light of the UN Convention for the Rights of the Child. The authors highlight the responsibilities of all adults who work with children, in terms of enabling children to realise their rights. The book includes chapters on inspection, equality, observation and assessment, parents and special needs, drawing on relevant theory and current research from the UK and overseas.

Written by key researchers and practitioners in the early childhood field, this book will help practitioners to appraise their practice; and provides insights for students on initial training courses and as part of continuing professional development.

'This text is recommended unreservedly; it should be on the bookshelves of all early childhood workers.'
CURRICULUM

1 85396 304 6   *Paperback*   144pp   1996

THREADS OF THINKING
Young Children Learning and the Role of Early Education
Cathy Nutbrown

This is a book for teachers in nursery and early education, and for other professional educators who wish to support and develop children's thinking. The author presents evidence of continuity and progression in young children's thinking and shows, with detailed observations, that young children are able and active learners. She considers aspects of children's patterns of learning and thinking – or schemas – and demonstrates clearly how children learn in an active, dynamic and creative way.

Numerous examples of young children 'in action' are used, which illustrate their learning in the areas of literacy, mathematics and science. Implications for the roles and responsibilities of educators, work with parents, and curriculum development are discussed.

User's Comments

'Clear description of aspects of cognitive development in young children, illustrated with examples from the author's research. Very useful for educators of the very young.'

1 85396 217 1   *Paperback*   176pp   1994